The
COLLABORATIVE
TEACHER

Working Together
as a Professional
Learning Community

D1417848

Cassandra Erkens

Chris Jakicic

Lillie G. Jessie

Dennis King

Sharon V. Kramer

Thomas W. Many

Mary Ann Ranells

Ainsley B. Rose

Susan K. Sparks

Eric Twadell

Solution Tree | Press

a division of
Solution Tree

Introduction by Richard DuFour   Foreword by Rebecca DuFour

555 North Morton Street
Bloomington, IN 47404
800.733.6786 (toll free) / 812.336.7700
FAX: 812.336.7790

email: info@solution-tree.com
solution-tree.com

Printed in the United States of America

13   12   11   10   5   6   7

FSC
Mixed Sources
Product group from well-managed
forests and other controlled sources
Cert no. SW-COC-002283
www.fsc.org
© 1996 Forest Stewardship Council

ISBN 978-1-934009-36-9

Solution Tree
Jeffrey C. Jones, CEO and President

Solution Tree Press
President: Douglas M. Rife
Publisher: Robert D. Clouse
Director of Production: Gretchen Knapp
Managing Production Editor: Caroline Wise
Cover Designer: Amy Shock

Other Resources on Professional Learning Communities

The Collaborative Administrator: Working Together as a Professional Learning Community

Getting Started: Reculturing Schools to Become Professional Learning Communities

A Leader's Companion: Inspiration for Professional Learning Communities at Work™

Learning by Doing: A Handbook for Professional Learning Communities at Work™

On Common Ground: The Power of Professional Learning Communities

Passion and Persistence: How to Develop a Professional Learning Community

The Power of Professional Learning Communities at Work™: Bringing the Big Ideas to Life

Professional Learning Communities at Work™: Best Practices for Enhancing Student Achievement

Professional Learning Communities at Work™ Plan Book

Pyramid Response to Intervention: RTI, PLCs, and How to Respond When Kids Don't Learn

Revisiting Professional Learning Communities at Work™: New Insights for Improving Schools

Through New Eyes: Examining the Culture of Your School

Whatever It Takes: How Professional Learning Communities Respond When Kids Don't Learn

Table of Contents

Foreword

Rebecca DuFour

In 1966, Seymour Sarason and his colleagues published "Teaching Is a Lonely Profession" in the book *Psychology in Community Settings: Clinical, Educational, Vocational, Social Aspects*. Sarason, considered to be one of the most significant researchers in education and educational psychology in the United States, concluded that teachers do most of their work in isolation, cut off from the support of colleagues with whom they should be linked. Almost 50 years later, despite the findings of numerous other organizational and educational researchers and the urgings of our professional organizations, we continue to struggle with overcoming the persistent norm of isolation in our profession.

We must acknowledge that no one person can or should be solely responsible for bringing about high levels of learning and tending to the diverse needs of each student. As the National Commission on Teaching and America's Future (2005) argues, to prepare students for success in the 21st century, we must develop the capacity of every teacher to "become members of a growing network of shared expertise."

When I first learned that 10 of our dear friends and highly respected colleagues were adding to the knowledge base in *The Collaborative Teacher*, I was delighted these educators were willing to share their expertise in such a lasting way. Prior to reading the chapters, I was confident each author was not only grounded in a solid understanding of educational best practices, but also brought years of rich experience as a practitioner who had applied the research in real classrooms, schools, and districts. After reading *The Collaborative*

Teacher, however, I must admit my delight has turned into elation as I realize the powerful contribution this book will make to our professional knowledge base regarding the benefits of working collaboratively rather than alone.

Chapter by chapter, the authors unwrap the big ideas of a professional learning community: 1) We embrace high levels of *learning* as our fundamental purpose; 2) we build a collaborative culture to ensure a collective response to learning needs; and 3) we use results—evidence of learning—to promote continuous improvement. The authors then present the reader with the gifts of understanding *why* collaboration is fundamental to our success as educators, *how* to collaborate in ways that directly impact student and adult learning, and *what* collaborative teams can do to take that learning to higher levels than ever before.

Readers will glean new insights and gather strategies for bringing collaboration to life as the authors demonstrate direct links between collaboration on the right topics and tasks to higher levels of learning. Readers will also reap the benefits of the authors' personal experiences and stories that affirm collaborative teachers touch the hearts and lives of students and their families in significant and lasting ways.

Educators who have had the good fortune of working in schools and districts where the norm of isolation is replaced with a new norm of collaboration would acknowledge the collaborative culture offers not only our best hope for improved learning for students and adults, but also for professional fulfillment. They have personal experience with Roland Barth's contention, "Teachers and students go hand in hand as learners—or they don't go at all" (2001, p. 23). I am so grateful to the dedicated educators and authors of *The Collaborative Teacher* for sharing their expertise as we continue to work together to transform the lonely *teaching* profession into the collaborative *learning* profession, working hand in hand to impact practice where it matters most—the heart of the school—the classroom.

References

Barth, R. (2001). *Learning by heart*. San Francisco: Jossey-Bass.

National Commission on Teaching and America's Future. (2005). *Induction into learning communities*. Washington, DC: Author. Accessed at http://www.nctaf. org/resources/research_and_reports/nctaf_research_reports/ on March 24, 2008.

Sarason, S., Levine, M., Goldenberg, I., Cherlin, D., & Bennett, E. (1966). *Psychology in community settings: Clinical, educational, vocational, social aspects*. San Francisco: John Wiley.

Introduction

Richard DuFour

When I began my teaching career 40 years ago, I had the good fortune to be 1 of 10 first-year teachers assigned to my high school. We neophytes bonded as we shared the experience of entering the profession. We became a de facto support group, turning to each other to express frustrations, to commiserate, or to decompress after a difficult day. Our relationships extended beyond the school. We socialized on a regular basis and even entered a team into an adult basketball league. We shared perceptions, emotions, and experiences.

Our sharing stopped, however, at our respective classroom doors, because within our classrooms, each of us reigned supreme. I never had to concern myself with what content others were teaching, because each of us was free to determine his or her own curriculum. There was no process, expectation, or even encouragement for me to discuss with colleagues my curriculum pacing, my instructional strategies, the methods and rigor of my assessments, my homework policy, my grading practices, my response to students who struggled, or any of the other vital issues essential to effective teaching. The only thing my sections of our U.S. history course had in common with the sections taught by others in my department was the title. Thus, the experience of students enrolled in the same course varied greatly because it was solely dependent upon the individual teacher to whom they had been randomly assigned.

Since each of us had complete authority to determine what occurred in our individual classrooms, we did not intrude upon one another's practice. We understood that to question a colleague's curricular or instructional decisions would represent a serious breach of teacher etiquette, an affront to his or her professional autonomy. To put it succinctly, we were *congenial* coworkers who worked in close proximity to one another, but we were never *colaborers*. None of us was a collaborative teacher.

Much has happened in education since then, but regrettably, even today many teachers continue to work in the same buffered isolation I experienced 4 decades ago. The good news, however, is that more and more teachers are working in schools in which collaborative cultures prevail. In these schools, teachers engage in collective inquiry on the questions most vital to student learning. They learn together, build shared knowledge, apply that knowledge to their classrooms, and then reflect on their experience to refine and improve their implementation. They clarify what their students must learn, systematically gather evidence of that learning through common formative assessments, and study the evidence together to inform and improve their individual and collective practice.

There are enormous differences between my experience and the workings of contemporary teachers working in powerful collaborative cultures. Whereas I defined my job as *teaching* (that is, presenting clear lessons), collaborative teachers accept responsibility for student *learning*. Not once in my entire teaching career was I ever called upon to present evidence of student learning beyond the grades I assigned. To this day I have no way of knowing whether I taught a skill or concept better or worse than my colleague across the hall. Collaborative teachers, on the other hand, are hungry for evidence of student learning. They create common formative assessments, analyze results together, and then use those results to help each other become more effective in their respective classrooms and to respond to the needs of individual students.

Whereas I worked in isolation, they work collaboratively. Whereas I worked independently to achieve my own goals, they work interdependently to achieve common goals for which they are mutually accountable. Whereas my colleagues and I understood, "These are *my* kids, and those are *your* kids," these teachers regard the success of every student as a collective responsibility: "These are all *our* students."

Researchers consistently report that the collaborative cultures created by these educators have helped students achieve at higher levels, fostered a powerful sense of professional efficacy among teachers, and made the teaching experience more rewarding and fulfilling. Almost all of the organizations representing educators have recognized the benefits of collaboration and have explicitly stated goals to support and advance the effort to make collaboration the norm in our schools and districts. That goal, however, remains elusive. In far too many schools, educators have been unable to overcome the tradition of isolation that, for over 40 years, has been cited as a major barrier to improving school effectiveness. In many other schools and districts, educators have settled for "collaboration lite." They don't build shared knowledge or collectively examine evidence of student learning; they share personal preferences ("This is how I like to teach this unit"). They don't concentrate on issues that can inform and improve their classroom practice; they discuss peripheral matters that have no direct impact on the classroom ("Who will distribute the field trip forms?").

The power of this book is not only that it calls upon teachers to collaborate, but that it also insists that they collaborate about the right things—the critical questions that lead to students learning at higher levels. These authors recognize the complexity of transforming school cultures to support professional collaboration, but they have faith in the ability of educators to make that transformation. They are highly successful school practitioners who offer the wisdom and insight that can only come with "learning by doing" in the real world of schools.

They provide a treasure trove of specific, practical, and proven strategies that can transform schools into places where every professional becomes the collaborative teacher.

Chapter Overview

In chapter 1, Cassandra Erkens asserts that teacher leaders play a key role in improving schools, and she calls upon all teachers to embrace the mantle of leadership. She defines the role of a teacher leader as collaborator, action researcher, reflective practitioner, and learner advocate. She offers brief vignettes that describe each role and then provides specific strategies to help educators build their capacity to assume each role.

In chapter 2, Susan Sparks tackles the issue of how teachers can begin to work together as members of a collaborative team when they have spent their careers working in isolation. She recognizes teachers will need support to make that transition, and she presents a rich array of structures and protocols to address both the "hardware" of a collaborative team (goals, products, strategies, and structures) as well as the "software" (beliefs, behaviors, relationships, and interpersonal effectiveness). She offers sound advice as to how educators can make their collaborative meetings positive and productive.

Tom Many devotes chapter 3 to examining the impact of a collaborative culture on professional practice in schools. More importantly, he identifies the specific high-leverage changes in practice that yield the greatest results. Psychologists have discovered that changing the way we talk can change the way we work (Kegan & Lahey, 2001). Tom illustrates that finding as he explores how the collaborative culture impacts the language that drives the work of a school. Finally, he affirms Michael Fullan's (2001) finding that the "single factor common to successful change initiatives is that relationships improve" (p. 5) by describing the impact of a powerful collaborative culture on the relationships of the professionals within a school. Tom uses survey results from principals and teachers throughout North America to illustrate his points in the words of educators themselves.

In chapter 4, Chris Jakicic emphasizes that a collaborative team of teachers cannot help all students learn unless they can agree on the answer to the question, "Learn what?" She reminds us of what educators throughout North America know to be true: It is impossible to ensure all students learn all that teachers have been asked to teach in the amount of time they have to teach it. She then provides specific suggestions regarding how a collaborative team can identify and focus upon the knowledge, skills, and dispositions most essential to the future success of their students. She illustrates how teachers can use the criteria established by Doug Reeves—endurance, leverage, and readiness for the next level of learning—to build the consensus essential to ensuring their students have access to a guaranteed curriculum that can be taught (and more importantly, learned) in the time available.

Eric Twadell explains in chapter 5 how members of a collaborative team can use the Japanese lesson study protocol to strengthen their curriculum, instruction, and relationships. Eric reviews the various elements of the protocols and then brings them to life through a story of a team's first attempt to use this powerful strategy. He points out that Japanese lesson study reinforces the collaboration, continuous improvement, focus on student learning, and job-embedded professional development characteristic of professional learning communities.

In chapter 6, Dennis King explores the inherent problems of both top-down and bottom-up school reform initiatives. He asserts that when teachers work collaboratively as members of a professional learning community, they can build the bridge that links broader school improvement initiatives with their daily practice in classrooms. Dennis uses the curriculum mapping process to illustrate how educators can align the intended curriculum created at the state or district level with the implemented curriculum that is presented in their classrooms each day. He then shares the insights of Rick Stiggins to help a collaborative team develop *quality* assessments that monitor student learning, inform teacher practice, and help students clarify where they must go next in their learning.

Lillie Jessie uses chapter 7 to point out the important distinction between *gathering* data and *using* data to respond to students in need and to improve professional practice. Lillie and her faculty have created a school where achievement data is easily accessible and openly shared, not only among members of a collaborative team, but also with the entire staff. She describes the seven stages her staff went through on their journey to build a collaborative culture that focuses evidence of student learning and the professional practices that impact that learning. Lillie acknowledges the many bumps in the road on that journey with wit, wisdom, and powerful analogies. She points out both the power and the need for celebrations along the way, and presents one of the most memorable lines in the book: "Toot your own horn, or it will remain in a state of untootedness."

All of the authors reference common assessments as an essential element in building professional learning communities, but in chapter 8, Ainsley Rose closely examines this powerful strategy for improving student achievement and promoting professional collaboration in detail. He begins by answering five critical questions posed by Rick Stiggins: What do we mean by *common*? What data should we collect? How will we use the data to inform our instructional decisions? Who will make the critical decisions about student learning? How can we involve students in the assessment process? Ainsley then explains a four-step process for teacher teams to create common assessments. He concludes that when teachers work through this process collaboratively, they enhance their effectiveness in the classroom and increase the likelihood of providing students with a high-quality guaranteed curriculum.

Sharon Kramer devotes chapter 9 to the issue that confronts—and befuddles—teachers throughout North America. At the end of virtually every unit of instruction, teachers discover some (probably most) students are proficient and ready to move forward with their learning, but some are not. What is the appropriate response? Sharon describes how teachers in a professional learning community work collaboratively and systematically to address this issue, rather than leaving the question for each teacher to resolve in isolation. She describes how teams use common preassessment and ongoing formative assessments to differentiate among students and then implement pyramids of intervention to provide additional time and support to students who have not learned. She then explains how those same teams also develop systems to enrich and extend the learning for students who are proficient. She acknowledges that these pyramids are not intended to substitute for effective instruction in the classroom each day, but rather to enhance that instruction through collaborative differentiation. Sharon concludes her chapter with stories illustrating how pyramids of intervention and enrichment are helping all students learn at higher levels, and then offers a very specific process teams can use to develop an integrated response to the learning needs of their students.

In the epilogue, Mary Ann Ranells offers the perspective of a former school administrator, district administrator, and high-ranking state department of education official who returned to the classroom as a teacher. She points out that the No Child Left Behind legislative mandate for "highly qualified teachers" emphasizes a myriad of qualifications for entering the classroom, but ignores the question of demonstrated effectiveness within the classroom. Mary Ann calls for teachers to move beyond the limits of "highly qualified" and to strive instead to become "spectacular" teachers. She then describes spectacular teachers as those who build relationships, collaborate with colleagues to build learning systems, redesign grading practices, wear multiple hats, and create a legacy for future generations. Most importantly, she provides techniques, strategies, and stories to help teachers move from qualified to spectacular.

I *highly* recommend this book as required reading for all educators attempting to break free of the debilitating tradition of professional isolation by developing their capacity to be contributing members of high-performing collaborative teams. Those who follow the wise counsel presented by these outstanding authors and work through the difficulties of implementation will make their schools wonderful places for learning—for students and the adults who serve them.

References

Kegan, R., & Lahey, L. (2001). *How the way we talk can change the way we work: Seven languages for transformation*. San Francisco: Jossey-Bass.

Fullan, M. (2001). *Leading in a culture of change*. San Francisco: Jossey-Bass.

Part One

WORKING TOGETHER FOR STUDENT LEARNING

CASSANDRA ERKENS

 An independent consultant and recognized leader in education, Cassandra Erkens shares her expert knowledge with teachers and administrators throughout the United States and Canada. Cassandra is the president of Anam Cara Consulting, Inc., and has served as a high school English teacher, district-level director of staff development, and state-level educational effectiveness regional facilitator. Cassandra has authored and coauthored several formal education-based training programs for Solution Tree and other national service providers. She trains all Solution Tree presenters, as well as other education experts.

ONE

The New Teacher Leader: Transforming Education From Inside the Classroom

Cassandra Erkens

In the past, the term *teacher leader* has been reserved for those of us who either have been advocates for our profession and our colleagues or have stepped out of the classroom to accept significant responsibilities for improving the system at large. Many of us, while teaching full time, have served as local union president, curriculum committee member, site leadership team chair, department chair, or grade-level team leader. Some of us have taken a temporary leave from our classrooms to serve as a teacher on special assignment: curriculum coordinator, instructional coach, literacy or math support team member, and other such system support roles. But unless we were willing to step *out* of our classrooms for these "extra" activities, we were seldom viewed as leaders in our field.

Thankfully, the work of professional learning communities (PLCs) is changing all that. As PLC architects DuFour and Eaker state, "Schools are effective because of their teachers, not in spite of them. . . . Situated in the classroom—the critical focal point of the learning community—teachers are essential to any meaningful reform effort and are in the best position to have a positive impact on the lives of children" (1998, p. 206). Today, teacher leaders must adopt a new frame of mind and a collaborative way of working to lead from *within* the classroom—the heart of change in education. To lead from the classroom in a manner that impacts student learning in significant ways, teacher leaders across North America are assuming four critical roles in their classrooms and with their learning communities: collaborator, action researcher, reflective practitioner, and learner advocate. Each role is unique, requiring its own set of skills.

The Collaborator

Jamie worked in a traditional high school that had not yet opted to operate as a professional learning community. Jamie's review of multiple research studies highlighted an overwhelmingly compelling argument that students and teachers alike would benefit if her math department created a collaborative culture. So, at the beginning of the school year, Jamie invited her department to consider operating as a PLC. Jamie had established a great rapport with her peers; they viewed her as a knowledgeable educator and outstanding teacher. Her colleagues were curious and intrigued by her findings, and because they trusted her, they readily agreed to follow her lead. They began by making the following commitments to each other:

- Make time to collaborate weekly, and commit to those established times.

- Bring best practice to their classrooms by researching and deciding as a team what to include and how.

- Identify the essential outcomes or power standards for each of their courses, put them in student-friendly language, and post them at the front of their classrooms.

- Co-create and implement common assessments to be used biweekly in the form of Monday quizzes and Friday tests tied directly to their posters of power standards.

- Codesign interventions and instructional strategies to address learner needs as determined by their common assessments.

- Commit to do whatever it takes to help all of their math learners.

The journey on which they embarked had its share of challenges, and the team truly had to work through some structural complications and philosophical differences. During difficult debates that drilled down to the core of their differing educational belief systems, Jamie was often certain everything would fold. When the team became tense and somewhat stuck, Jamie worked one on one with team members to identify their hurdles and discover how she could best help them overcome barriers and trust the ideas of their peers long enough to try new things.

By the end of the first semester, the math department had dramatically reduced the failure rate in courses that used common assessments, moving from the traditional bell curve 30% failure rate to a low 5% failure rate. Surprisingly, even team members who had not yet used common assessments experienced some of this success in their courses. During the team's discussion of the results, these teachers noted that while they hadn't used common assessment data to inform their instructional planning, they had, in fact, altered their responses, adopting a "whatever it takes" approach to require student learning in their classrooms.

The math department's overall success was cause for celebration. Jamie celebrated the work of the team internally and externally. As a result, the team renewed their commitments to collaborate as a way of continuously improving their student achievement results.

What We Know About Collaboration

Teacher leaders understand that the work of teaching is far too complex and the work of learning is far too important for us to confine student achievement within the limitations of our personal expertise. Hence, we choose to lead our peers in meaningful and even challenging collaboration in order to address the needs of our learners. Teacher leaders like Jamie can elicit collaboration from colleagues because they are able to establish a high level of trust and rapport with the team.

Collaboration is founded on trust. In their long-term work with schools, sociologists and authors Bryk and Schneider (2002) identified four critical pillars to support trust in schools: respect, competence, integrity, and personal regard for others. These characteristics are not new, but they can seem rare and appear to be intuitive to the leaders we respect and willingly follow. These four critical pillars require intentionality and commitment—even tenacity. They must be collectively defined and collaboratively practiced in community. Trust in a team is jeopardized when members hold fast to autonomy and self-select the responsibilities, conversations, or values to which they will commit. We *require* the participation and expertise of the *entire team* when working collaboratively. So, in a professional learning community *all* staff must understand and develop these leadership characteristics.

Respect

Strong teacher leaders know to build relationships. They understand that rapport begins with respect. They respect others and are in turn respected because they know that "the success or failure of teacher leaders will depend on their relationships with their colleagues" (Johnson & Donaldson, 2007, p. 13). Teacher leaders are clear that who they are as the messenger is as important as the message they carry. Colleagues will not hear them if they are not both respected and respectful.

Because respect is a critical element in building a truly collaborative team, teacher leaders do not leave it to chance. It must be discussed as a team. When teams establish norms, the word *respect* is invariably someplace on the list:

- We will respect each other.

- We will respect our differences.

- We will demonstrate respectful behaviors throughout our meetings.

But this term is completely subjective, and when left undefined by a team, *respect* becomes the cornerstone of future disagreement: "You said we should respect our differences, but here you are challenging my classroom practices!"

Does respect mean absolute acceptance? When using such value-laden terms, teacher leaders take the direct approach of helping the team clarify both what the term looks like and what it does not look like by using "what if" scenarios: "What would it look like if we were being respectful of individual differences but still pushed on each other's thinking until we could come to consensus on an issue?" But defining respect is simply the beginning. The practice of a norm such as respect involves focused effort and ongoing discussion. Inevitably, we will need additional clarification. To prepare for such trial-and-error incidents, teacher leaders help the team strategize ahead of time the best way to address any experience that violates the team norm: "Let's agree that if we are concerned about the potential violation of a norm, we will address it promptly during the meeting by simply asking the team for a norm check and clarification." Respect is far too important for team success to be left to individual interpretations.

Competence

In her book *Trust Matters: Leadership for Successful Schools* (2004), author Megan Tschannen-Morgan defines competence as "the ability to perform a task as expected, according to appropriate standards" (p. 30). She further states, "In schools, principals and teachers depend upon one another's competence to accomplish the teaching and learning goals of the school" (p. 30). Competence involves the application of knowledge and skills consistently over time.

Educators have always been able to identify peers who demonstrate high levels of competence through content mastery and instructional prowess. In an effort to assert competence among peers, some staff will leverage the sheer volume (in quantity and vocif-

erousness!) of their concerns as a means to mask their own resistance. But that strategy is detrimental as the pattern quickly becomes
transparent.

Competent teachers are as willing to challenge as they are to be
challenged. Often we appreciate the quiet competence demonstrated
by the reflective peer who asks open, honest questions to enhance his
own understanding and practice. His questions are a hallmark of his
strength, not his weakness; "we trust people whose skill we depend
upon, especially professionals, to be honest about their level of skill
and to maintain their skills" (Tschannen-Morgan, 2004, p. 31). We
do not just follow a colleague's lead because his competence is compelling; no one is interested in following a know-it-all who offers a
steady diet of what others "should" do! We are grateful to the competent teacher who acknowledges the team's areas for growth, who
makes himself a learner alongside his team members, and who holds
himself and everyone on the team accountable to addressing the gap.
We welcome the peer who demonstrates a commitment to excellence in his field by freely volunteering high-quality models of the
very characteristics, strategies, and tools he advocates others employ.
Competent teachers might not view themselves as leaders, but they
are the first to whom we turn for ready resources, new ideas, and
trusted problem-solving support. They are leaders by the nature of
their own responsiveness and ability to help.

Integrity

In the book *Influencer: The Power to Change Anything* (2007), the
authors assert that those who influence others have not only proven
themselves trustworthy and competent, but "they also have other
people's best interest in mind. This means that they aren't seen as
using their knowledge to manipulate or harm, but rather to help"
(Patterson et al., p. 153). True leaders operate with integrity. The
teacher leaders we choose to follow exude integrity in every way.
Teacher leaders with integrity are committed to excellence, refusing

to make decisions based on the limitations of contractual agreements. They never sacrifice quality for personal ease.

But professional integrity demands much more than commitment to hard work and long days; it also challenges us to explore the complexities and the nuances of teaching by refining our craft and coalescing our efforts into educational practices that guarantee student achievement. Teacher leaders with integrity integrate standards, assessment, instruction, and classroom management into a seamless, powerful learning experience for all students. Teaching is a profession that can never be perfected, but teacher leaders never give up, because it is a calling that can never be neglected. With integrity, teacher leaders work to help all of us refine our craft.

Personal Regard for Others

Teaming can be fraught with challenges, and teachers generally enter collaborative work with eyes wide open to potential frustrations. While this fear can certainly deter motivation and commitment, team members will follow a teacher leader for whom they have personal regard because they anticipate that her skill and competence will help them overcome hurdles safely. Trust is built even more quickly when team members know the respected leader holds each of them in high esteem as well: "Respect gives people the self-confidence to take risks in making decisions" (Tichy & Cardwell, 2004, p. 83). The safety of such knowledge empowers teams to take risks and become learners in their own process. With the right leader, a team can foresee a successful outcome as a given, since even a failed outcome would be deemed just another growth opportunity.

A team is part of a larger system and teacher leaders demonstrate personal regard for all stakeholders in team decisions. There can be no room for "we versus they" language: "We wouldn't have to do this if the administration just trusted us," or "Those demanding parents and students are making our jobs more challenging than need be."

To view collaboration as something that only happens inside a team is to be short-sighted about the long-term health of the team. The entire system must work together. Strong teacher leaders identify and protect the needs of all stakeholders.

The Leader as One of the Team

Establishing trust is foundational for the work of collaboration, but it is only a means to an end and not the end itself. Teams collaborate to address curriculum issues, to create common assessments, to explore effective intervention strategies, and so on. To collaborate is to co-create strategies and actions together. Teacher leaders like Jamie might help to lead the team in the right direction, but they also function as a member of the team. This means they facilitate collaborative ventures *knowing* they cannot predetermine answers for their peers. They ask the right questions, but they are careful not to have all the answers along the way. Their success will depend on whether or not they can empower the team to address emerging needs and resolve issues together.

Moreover, teacher leaders work to help all members become leaders as well:

> To create organizations that get smarter and more aligned every day requires an interactive teaching/learning process. It isn't hierarchical teaching. You teach me, and then I teach the people below me. It isn't about alternating roles. You teach me something and then I'll teach you something. Rather, it is a process of mutual exploration and exchange during which both the "teacher" and the "learner" become smarter. It is synergy. 1 + 1 = 3. (Tichy & Cardwell, 2004, p. 10)

A learner amongst peers, teacher leaders leverage collaboration to create the synergy needed for teams to respond to each new challenge they encounter.

The Action Researcher

Miguel, a middle school teacher, was frustrated. It seemed to him that as soon as he evaluated his students' writing assignments, learning ended; students simply accepted their grades, without trying to revise or improve their work. Miguel searched through educational books and journals and found many educational theorists who agreed that the traditional grading system is problematic, but he could not find any solutions.

One day he stumbled upon a new book that offered some tangible solutions. Excited, Miguel brought the book to his seventh-grade language arts team to share its ideas. The team agreed that they needed help answering the question, "How can we develop a grading system that increases motivation and encourages continued learning for middle-school students in language arts?" They agreed to spend a trimester's worth of action research answering this question.

Together the team mapped out some innovative strategies for managing grades within their classrooms and then created some tools and processes for monitoring student learning and motivation with the new system. They consistently documented their findings, tracking the results for a full semester. At the end of the first trimester, they reviewed the final findings, and each team member unequivocally agreed that the new system was far superior in encouraging learning and motivation, but a bit time-consuming and "clunky," as one team member put it, for the day-to-day management of the actual student grades. The team decided to continue the action research and spent the second trimester on refining their grading tools and processes. As before, they monitored the overall effectiveness of their efforts along the way.

What We Know About Action Research

Educational experts in the field acknowledge that it is not enough to simply accept the best practices outlined in their own theories and research. Such experts encourage us to implement their ideas within our own classrooms, to generate our own evidence of how high-yield, best-practice strategies work with *our* kids, *our* state standards, *our* school, and so on. This process is called *action research.*

Action research is an applied and disciplined inquiry process that helps educators "be more effective at what they care most about—their teaching and the development of their students" (Sagor, 2000, p. 3). Action research is a powerful model for professional development that allows teachers to learn from concrete, *local* evidence what works and what does not work in their classrooms. A teacher leader willing to invest in the process of action research to test a new classroom strategy, for example, will always move beyond the surface level understanding that he might gain during a staff in-service. Because he monitors the effectiveness of the practice by collecting evidence from his classroom, he practices and refines the strategy over time, leading to deep implementation of any strategy that works.

Teacher leaders like Miguel don't just dare to challenge the status quo of the system at large; they challenge the status quo of their own practice, by seeking the areas that need improvement. Focused on the outcome of improved student learning, teacher leaders integrate inquiries into their practice, gather evidence to evaluate their effectiveness, and alter their practices to accommodate their new understanding. Often, they share their results with colleagues so others might benefit from their findings.

While it is entirely possible for a teacher to conduct action research in his classroom without the participation of his peers, a strong teacher leader will find a way to engage his colleagues in participating in the research process. He understands that a collective approach to each step of the process—framing the question, solving problems, generating common data, and interpreting results—will produce more accurate results and have a far greater impact on student learning in many classrooms. Through our action research, we create a true learning organization. Action research becomes the new standard procedure for how we respond to recommended and research-based educational practices.

The Reflective Practitioner

Even though Yanni was widely recognized by her peers as an exceptional teacher, she knew she had room for growth. Since she had never felt particularly strong when it came to teaching social studies in her third-grade classroom, she never enjoyed teaching that subject—and she was pretty sure her students weren't enjoying her teaching of it, either! Yanni decided she was going to have to do something in her own classroom in the area of social studies for the benefit of her learners and for her own comfort and confidence.

Yanni's school had been functioning as a professional learning community for quite some time. In the absence of the common assessment data that Yanni had grown to trust, she laid her first-quarter grades in social studies next to the first-quarter grades of her peers. On first glance, there were no striking irregularities, but as Yanni thought about it, she realized those data were relative to her classroom expectations, and she would need to dig deeper to explore the content quality and quantity from room to room. With all of their energies targeting literacy (the SMART goal for their school), her team had not yet identified their power standards for social studies, but Yanni decided to get started anyway.

In looking over her peers' lists of outcomes and curriculum plans for the first quarter, Yanni quickly discovered that while everyone covered the same general topics, her peers were covering them at deeper levels than she was. Their plans required students to develop reasoning patterns and linked lessons to the larger processes and concepts of social studies (such as, "Patterns repeat themselves between and among cultures and over time"). Yanni had the same grade distribution because her kids were answering her test questions accurately, but she realized that neither her questions nor her expectations had the rigor of her peers'. Yanni needed to act immediately to improve her own skill and understanding in social studies instruction because her learners deserved better. She began by brainstorming the strategies that would best help her improve:

- Exploring national standards to understand the larger concepts and processes of social studies

- Aligning her curriculum outcomes to the state standards and the performance expectations of her peers by seeking their counsel

- Studying research-based instructional strategies

- Integrating reasoning patterns into her lessons and assessments

While she hasn't yet mastered the art of teaching social studies, Yanni is satisfied that she is making significant strides, and she's no longer as worried about the welfare of her students. She plans to invite her team to include social studies in their PLC efforts.

What We Know About Reflective Practice

Reflective practitioners have a strong sense of their personal strengths and learning curves, but they take it one step further and seek confirmation of their strengths in student results. They set aside personal defensiveness regarding past efforts and preconceived notions of what may or may not work regarding future efforts. A reflective person might spend considerable time pondering her effectiveness, but a reflective *practitioner* seeks answers outside of herself and takes action to address her gaps. A strong teacher leader acknowledges the ruts of long-term patterns and recognizes the limitations of her own thinking. Given that, she accepts that her efforts to understand anything deeply will require her to re-examine her practices, her beliefs, and her results—for new insight cannot emerge from staid assumptions. She regularly opens herself to both risk and learning.

Today's teacher leaders are *learning* leaders. They attend not only to the results of their efforts (achievement of results), but also to the quality of their inputs (antecedents of excellence) that lead to the results (Reeves, 2006). Teacher leaders diligently study the research, their current practices, and the impact of their efforts on student learning. They employ reflection as an active, conscious process of carefully reviewing an experience or a new idea. They define, analyze, synthesize, and evaluate their practice and beliefs, and hence create new insight and collective understanding. Reflection in the classroom serves as the means by which strong teachers verify that they possess the professional competencies (knowledge, skills, attitudes, and beliefs) necessary for teaching effectively. Teacher leaders are reflective practitioners, committing themselves to continuous improvement in the art and science of teaching.

The Learner Advocate

Takoda was in his fourth year of teaching in a district with a high rate of student absenteeism and dropout. He had noticed that his peers believed the students in this district, situated in a community with relatively low socioeconomic status, were already doing the best they could. Staff felt significantly handicapped when it came to dealing with the issues their students faced outside of the schools: poverty, high drug and alcohol use, and low parent involvement.

But Takoda had experienced a teacher who hadn't given up on him while he was growing up, and he understood firsthand what a difference a teacher could make. In his classroom, he was relentless about helping students learn to high levels of achievement, and as a result, his students experienced success. He had come to believe, however, that improving learning in one classroom was not enough. Takoda decided it was time to address the student achievement gaps on the school and possibly even the district level.

Takoda realized he had to begin by changing staff perception of their students. He believed their students were more than simply unmotivated statistics. He visited with his principal and requested the opportunity to seek the data on the students they were losing academically. The principal responded that he already had the data and provided Takoda with spreadsheets full of statistics on the socioeconomic status, ethnicity, average home life situation, grade point average, and so on. When Takoda pressed that having this data did not mean they fully knew or understood the learners or their needs, the principal said research suggested that students within these certain populations typically behaved in the same way as their own students. After some discussion, he offered Takoda the opportunity to get the information he insisted was missing.

To get started, Takoda gathered the students who frequently skipped school and conducted focus groups seeking to learn what they found exciting about school, what strengths they brought to their learning experience, what got in the way of their success in school, what they needed to remain connected to the school, and so on. He also interviewed some of the district's dropout students. His findings clearly indicated that they could be doing more on a school and district basis to help their learners be more successful. Students shared the following insights:

- Classes and assignments were redundant and boring. In some cases, students were asked to read the same book three different times in their educational journey.

- Teachers were rigid and did not allow for mistakes or misunderstandings. It was not safe to ask questions if a student did not grasp the concept or the assignment the first time.

- In many classes, two missed assignments equated to irreversible doom on the report card.

Ninety-five percent of the students had no hope of reversing the downward spiral in their academic achievement. In fact, many of them could no longer find their own strengths or talents to call upon in other difficult situations, so giving up had become their only option—creating a self-perpetuating cycle of failure.

Takoda shared his results with staff. The issues that emerged were far more complex and reproving of schools than the adults' simple descriptors and easily applied explanations of students as nonresponsive, lazy, or unable to learn on the basis of negative societal influences. With Takoda's revealing findings in hand, staff began to discuss how they could improve the student-identified concerns within the staff's control to impact student learning in positive ways.

What We Know About Learner Advocacy

Teacher leaders believe the burden of responsibility for educating all students rests squarely on the shoulders of the system, and they neither accept doom nor await the liberator in shining armor to lead them to solutions: "Effective teachers . . . see themselves as responsible for student learning. They do not perceive learning problems as products of students' personal backgrounds, but rather as indications that adaptations need to be made in instructional approach so that learning can take place. These teachers believe in their ability to reach and teach virtually all of their students successfully" (Cotton, 2001). Teacher leaders are adamant about serving as advocates for all of our learners, helping us move beyond stigmas and labels, outdated "research," and even our comfort zones to change the system.

As learner advocates, teachers approach their students with a "growth mindset": They share with their students "the love of challenge, belief in effort, resilience in the face of setbacks, and greater (more creative) success" (Dweck, 2006, p. 12). They accept the challenge of helping every student on an individual basis, including students with whom they struggle to build relationships. Demonstrating healthy self-awareness of their strengths and limitations, biases and misunderstandings, learner advocates persevere. They are resilient. In difficult situations, they consult the wisdom of experts, solicit the expertise of their peers, and engage their own creativity and reflective practice to meet the needs of *each* learner within their classrooms. They believe the journey is worth the effort for both student and teacher alike.

Like Takoda, today's teacher leader challenges deficit thinking. He does not see the learner as "at risk," but rather as "with potential." In research conducted with a variety of minority populations, Robert Sternberg, cognitive psychologist, researcher, teacher and author, discovered that "students in underrepresented minority groups have culturally relevant knowledge and diverse cognitive abilities that schools can use to promote learning" (Sternberg, 2006, p. 30). Believing that to be true, strong teacher leaders work to identify and leverage each learner's assets, drawing on their tacit knowledge, cultural heritage, unique interests, desires, learning styles, and intelligences. Through building relationships with all of their students, these teachers create a rich learning environment of relevance and rigor.

An Integrated Approach

It might seem overwhelming or unrealistic that a teacher leader could simultaneously play all four roles: collaborator, action researcher, reflective practitioner, and learner advocate. And yet each of the four roles defined in this chapter engages teachers in similar processes to create and maintain the characteristics of professional learning communities:

- Shared mission, vision, values, goals

- Collaborative teams

- Collective inquiry

- Action orientation and experimentation

- Commitment to continuous improvement

- Results focus (DuFour & Eaker, 1998)

Those teachers who lead us in transforming education from inside the classroom readily move in and out of the four roles—developing and implementing all the skills and processes that are required to fill their mission of high levels of student achievement. They empower themselves and their peers. They create an environment of hopefulness. They generate a sense of efficacy.

Today's teacher leaders are exemplary in their commitment to their calling, they are passionate in their drive for excellence, and they are inspiring in their willingness, even eagerness, to transform their own classrooms and personal practice as they work daily to transform the lives of our students. It is only from such classrooms that the very idea of school reform is even possible.

References

Bryk, A., & Schneider, B. (2002). *Trust in schools: A core resource for improvement.* American Sociological Association Rose Series. New York: Russell Sage Foundation.

Cotton, K. (2001). *Educating urban minority youth: Research on effective practices.* Northwest Regional Educational Laboratory. School Improvement Research, Topical Synthesis No. 4. Accessed at www.nwrel.org/scpd/sirs/5/topsyn4.html on October 16, 2007.

DuFour, R., & Eaker, R. (1998). *Professional learning communities at work: Best practices for enhancing student achievement.* Bloomington, IN: Solution Tree (formerly National Educational Service).

Dweck, C. (2006). *Mindset: The new psychology of success.* New York: Random House.

Johnson, S., & Donaldson, M. (2007). Overcoming the obstacles to leadership. *Educational Leadership, 65*(1), 8–13.

Patterson, K., Grenny, J., Maxfield, D., McMillan, R., & Switzler, A. (2007). *Influencer: The power to change anything.* New York: McGraw-Hill.

Reeves, D. (2006). *The learning leader: How to focus school improvement for better results.* Alexandria, VA: Association for Supervision and Curriculum Development.

Sagor, R. (2000). *Guiding school improvement with action research.* Alexandria, VA: Association for Supervision and Curriculum Development.

Sternberg, R. (2006). Recognizing neglected strengths. *Educational Leadership, 64*(1), 30–35.

Tichy, N., & Cardwell, N. (2004). *The cycle of leadership: How great leaders teach their companies to win.* New York: Harper Business.

Tschannen-Morgan, M. (2004). *Trust matters: Leadership for successful schools.* San Francisco: Jossey-Bass.

SUSAN K. SPARKS

 Susan K. Sparks is an educational consultant and executive director of the Front Range Board of Cooperative Educational Services (BOCES) for Teacher Leadership, which serves 19 member school districts in the Denver metro region. The BOCES works in partnership with the School of Education at the University of Colorado at Denver with the single purpose of improving student learning through collaborative professional development. Susan has been an educational leader in Colorado for over 20 years and has facilitated multiple initiatives and collaborative projects. Her passion for empowering educators is evident in every aspect of her work. Known as a results-oriented facilitator, she coordinates ongoing statewide professional learning community institutes, assists district administration, schools, and teams through transition and change, and consults in community building, planning, and conflict resolution.

TWO

Creating Intentional Collaboration

Susan K. Sparks

What is worth fighting for is not to allow our schools to be negative by default, but to make them positive by design.

—Michael Fullan and Clif Germain

Have you had a negative experience being on a team? Recall the team, how you felt, and what behaviors you noticed from yourself and all those around you. How many of the following behaviors look familiar?

- Attending without bringing necessary items to the meeting

- "Checking out" or focusing on unrelated tasks

- Discussing the same issue or student over and over

- Listening to one or two people doing most of the talking

- Complaining about the administration or district mandates

- Lamenting the lack of clear directions about the work

- Dismissing or demeaning others' points of view

- Withholding opinions during the meeting and talking afterward in the hallway, lounge, or parking lot

- Leaving the meeting without closure and a plan

If you found yourself relating to this list, you may have also noticed that poorly designed and unproductive team meetings create ripples through a school and create negative and unintended consequences. Conversations focus less on student learning and more on adult behaviors. Relationships become tentative and fragile. Few changes occur, and the end result of poor meetings is lack of trust, overt resistance, and disenfranchised teachers who see no value in the collaborative team process.

This scenario does not have to be your reality if you are thoughtful and intentional about the process of working together. Think about a team you have been part of that is truly collaborative and focused on student learning. You may have seen the following behaviors:

- Clarifying both purpose and goal at the start of the meeting
- Filling important roles such as facilitating and recording
- Using an agenda to stay focused on the meeting's purpose
- Attending to the task at hand and fully participating
- Using processes to discuss topics, gather information, analyze, and make decisions
- Listening and learning from diverse points of view
- Praising and congratulating one another
- Doing the work in the room, during the meeting
- Tackling tough issues
- Calling one another's attention to the norms
- Leaving knowing what is expected to prepare for the next meeting

Relationships on these teams are professional, and everyone is focused on student learning. There is a feeling of personal responsibility and a "can do" attitude from members. Positive energy creates ripples throughout the school, and it moves staff, students, and community to greater achievement and results. Teachers value their time together, and positive momentum occurs before, during, and after collaborative time.

You have the choice to become either one of these teams. Professional learning communities are built on the foundation of collaborative teams as interdependent, self-directed work groups focused on a common goal. Bossidy and Charan (2002) describe this balance between task and relationship in teams as the "hardware and software" of teams. They suggest that "the hardware of a computer is useless without the right software. Similarly, in an organization the hardware (strategy and structure) is inert without the software (beliefs and behaviors)" (p. 85). For some, the hardware is the "what" or the task. It is also the goal, the membership, the structures, and the time. The software may be the interpersonal effectiveness and trustworthiness of team members—the relationships. This chapter will highlight both hardware and software necessary for effective team meetings to show what works to build a high-performing team. You will learn how your contributions can play a pivotal role in your team's success. You can inspire others through leading by example.

Five Keys to Successful Team Meetings

To be successful, teachers should examine their team practice around five key elements of effective team meetings:

1. Focus

2. Roles and responsibilities

3. Structure

4. Process

5. Behaviors and relationships

The Team Meeting Organizer (page 35) provides a working tool to help you plan and address each of these components. Each element of the Organizer is described in detail in this chapter. Use it! Keep it front and center and refer to it throughout your meeting. Think of the Organizer as a lesson plan focused on results for your team. It takes a little time initially to work through, but teams that use it believe in its value. We know it is worth spending time planning to create a successful team experience; commit to using the tools and strategies described under each component in your meetings, and observe what works. There is not a perfect formula for what to do during your first team meeting, your second meeting, and so on. Just begin. Work together and talk out loud as you go. As you meet and work, you will learn more. You will continue to ask, "What do we need to do next?" Talking through the Team Meeting Organizer will help you design your next work session and stay focused on the work.

1. Focus

The professional learning community model has helped shift the focus of teams from casual conversations about individual students and climate issues to rich dialogue about student learning. Teams work together to create essential learnings, guaranteed and viable curriculum, formative and summative common assessments, and interventions, all for the purpose of improving student learning.

Because the focus of meetings is more intentional in a PLC, collaborative team meetings become a place where teachers successfully tackle the complex work of educating all students to high levels of learning. Under the heading of "Focus" on the Team Meeting Organizer are listed the following topics: SMART Goals, Purpose and Non-Purpose, Results, Objectives and Products, Linking, and Clarifying and Checking Perceptions.

SMART Goals

Your team must have a SMART goal. The goal is substantiated by data reflecting your current reality and a specific target area where your students need to improve. This goal becomes the end statement and what you aspire to. It is the reason your team exists. Your team goal must be explicit and agreed upon, and it must relate to improved student learning by directly contributing to the school goal or school

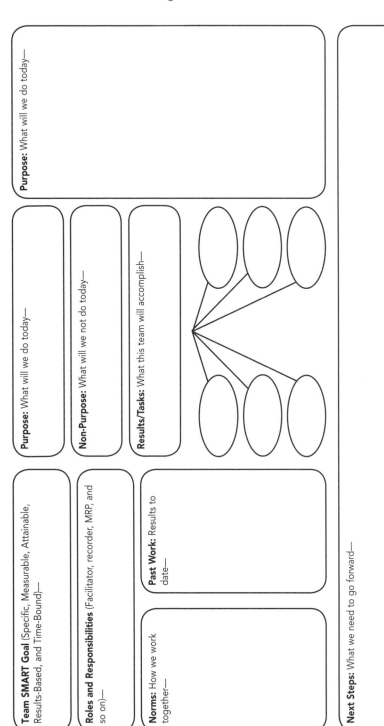

Figure 2-1. Team Meeting Organizer (*Adapted from Centennial BOCES, 2002.*)

improvement goal. After analysis and hard conversation, your team works in collaboration with your principal to reach consensus and begins. Your team takes action now!

School Goal Example

87% of students in grades 3–5 will score at either a proficient or advanced level of performance in writing as measured by the 2008 CSAP.

100% of students in grades K–5 will score proficient as measured by the district writing assessment by May 2008.

Team Goal Example

The power of the team goal is to remind us of our progress toward the school goal and provide opportunity to reflect and adjust instruction or content. The team goal supports the school goal and is based on specific and unique needs of the students.

By the end of January 2008, 90% of 4th-grade students will score at or above proficient in writing organization and conventions as measured by district level assessments.

Purpose

The school and team goal is the focus. However, it will not describe what you do each time you meet. The purpose is a statement of what you will accomplish during each team meeting. Examples of purpose statements include:

- "Today we will review our essential skills in writing and determine if they are still relevant and essential."

- "Today we are going to write student-friendly learning targets in seventh-grade mathematics."

- "Our purpose is to determine interventions for students not reading at grade level."

Every time you meet, a purpose statement needs to be expressed and written on the Team Organizer. If it is not evident what the purpose is, say out loud to your colleagues, "What are we focused on today? What do we want to accomplish?" or "Okay . . . where are we headed today?"

Non-Purpose

If you think team members are expecting something different from the meeting or have a hidden agenda, it may be beneficial to state the non-purpose of the meeting. Using non-purpose is a preventative strategy for being drawn off task. Statements should be framed in the positive. However, you may find yourself expressing non-negotiables or at least declarative statements in a way that describes "what we will not do." Examples of statements of non-purpose might be as follows:

- "Our non-purpose today is to backtrack and talk about why we are implementing professional learning communities."

- "Our non-purpose is to discuss individual student issues today."

- "Our non-purpose is to map out the upcoming unit. Remember, we have time for that on Thursday."

When you deliver a non-purpose, use a gentle and firm voice. This will allow the group to release some of their anxiety and focus on the task at hand.

Evaluation and Results

Along with determining how to track the goal and collect the data to support achievement of the goal, your team needs to think about evaluation and results. What tangible results will you have from your work together? Sometimes your work is defined in the parameters and non-negotiables from the school leadership team or principal. If not, make sure to describe, with specifics, what your outcome will look like. Ask, "What happened as a result of our work? Did students achieve and perform? What evidence do we have?" The best results are increased student performance and learning. However, teams also need to see short-term results and concrete products as they work toward improving student learning.

Objectives and Products

In your Organizer, write the specific objectives of the meeting. Capture the team's ideas in the planning bubbles. It may be one big idea with several details, or it may be specific products captured in the bubbles. Tom Many, Superintendent of Kildeer Countryside Community Consolidated School District 96, encourages his teams to make their work real by writing a clear description or producing something tangible. Teams live by the mantra, "If it isn't written down, it doesn't exist." Many argues that if an idea can't be communicated in writing or with some kind of diagram or visual, there is still more clarification and work to be done to create mutual understanding. Team members benefit from shared meaning and creating tangible products together. It is important that teams have a clear picture of what they are working towards for each session. Examples of products include development of a writing rubric, a common assessment for an end of a unit, a definition of what constitutes a good intervention, a curriculum map for Algebra 1, and parental pamphlet describing departmental grading policies. This step will help you clarify what you specifically want to achieve during your time together.

Linking

Teachers are busy and move from one task to another, often multitasking in the same meeting! Sometimes it is difficult to remember what happened from one meeting to the next. It is good to remind yourselves of accomplishments and progress so far. Your team should link the purpose of each meeting to your past work; describe how much progress was made or what results occurred. The Team Organizer has a bubble for describing past work.

To link to the past, you might say:

- "Remember what we did last time we met? We reviewed research describing the value of professional learning communities and discussed the six essential elements."

- "The question we addressed last time we met was, 'Do professional learning communities make a difference in student achievement?'"

- "Last time we were together, we saw wonderful summary statements in our student writing."

To link to the future, make notes in the bubble for Next Meeting Focus. You may use statements like, "Remember, in a month, we need to turn in essential learning targets for our course," or, "Next week we will be reviewing our student achievement data and looking at the state and district results."

This technique is called linking past, present, and future, and it grounds your entire team. It helps you celebrate good work and creates awareness of your past productivity and the expectation that your productivity will continue and you will achieve results. Linking contributes to purposeful and intentional work.

Clarifying and Checking Perceptions

When you first begin, and throughout at periodic intervals, it is important to ask boundary questions such as, "Are we working within our parameters? What is our authority? What is our charge?" If you are not clear, ask your administrator. Do not hesitate to express that you want to do your best work and need a little more information and clarification. Effective teams check in the beginning, and they check as they go. Clarifying increases communication and ownership. It is good practice to share your understanding "out loud" and request guidance and advice.

Teams may stop work (or not even begin) if they are confused about the task and products. Sometimes, however, this confusion is actually a politically correct form of resistance. Don't let "confusion" derail your committee. If the roles and tasks are unclear, go ask your principal!

If your principal gives you his or her best answer and it is still muddy, jump in and begin anyway. Sometimes, work is not clear and a little—or a lot—messy. Start working. After you have accomplished something and started the process, go back to your principal and ask if this seems to be on track and what advice might he or she give you as you move forward.

Do not be the team that hesitates or actually resists doing something because of confusion. Try to complete some or all of the Focus bubbles on your Team Organizer, but do not get stuck overanalyzing and planning without action. Mike Schmoker (2006) warns us that spending too much time in planning will undo our best efforts. Upon his review of school improvement plans, he maintains that on close examination, lengthy, ambiguously worded documents wreak havoc (Schmoker, 2006). Be clear and purposeful. Take time up front, but do not get bogged down.

You should create your agenda only after identifying the SMART goal, purpose, non-purpose, linking, and results. This leads us to important questions. Who takes initiative for determining goals and purpose? Who creates the agenda? How does this happen?

2. Roles and Responsibilities

Formally naming team leaders, chairs, or facilitators helps the team move quickly. If your principal has not done this, ask, "What process would you recommend to define leadership roles in our team?" If the principal asks the team to decide, *decide.* Do not let this question go unasked and the task therefore undone.

Lack of planning, fuzzy goals, and unclear process can slow your team down for months and set you on a path of confusion and disillusionment. If your team needs to decide how you will work, suggest at your first meeting, "This is what I know about why we are meeting. We are being asked to create a collaborative team to impact student learning, so we need to be clear on our goal. I also think it will take work to organize. Is anyone willing to help us begin, define our task, and facilitate our first few meetings?"

If one of your teammates steps up, express you have an interest, too, and suggest you tag team. If no one volunteers, you might say, "I have an interest, and if you will help me think through the focus of our work, I will facilitate for a while." Here is your chance to learn more about leadership and facilitation and make a positive difference!

The typical roles within a collaborative team include facilitator, recorder, group member, and most responsible person (MRP). There are many more roles in teams too numerous to mention here. Consider the following, and commit to learning more.

Facilitator

The facilitator will help the team move forward and create results. This role can be shared, but whoever wears the facilitator hat must manage the process and ensure there is a beginning, middle, and end to each work session.

All members of the team should have opportunities for balanced input. Pay attention to managing one topic and one process at a time (Garmston & Wellman, 1999). The facilitator guides the team's work and makes things easy for the team. Facilitators often design the meeting and bring data for team discussion. Some schools and districts are providing accessible data and even arranging it for their teams, in which case the facilitator helps the data become public and used during team meetings.

Recorder

The recorder does the charting and note-taking for the team. Your team will need to decide how much to record, but the rule of thumb is to describe the purpose, what was accomplished, what was decided, next steps, and who will do it. It is also important to note what the team wants to do at the next meeting.

Some teams do not take minutes, but the facilitator will still need to track the work. This record becomes critical to linking to the next meeting and keeping the group on track. Legacy High School in Adams Twelve Five-Star School District in Broomfield, Colorado, uses an electronic reporting tool to report results and keep minutes. This tool provides focus and public record of each team's work.

Group Member

Effective group members stay conscious of their actions and behaviors in the meeting. They participate and use effective communication skills. A member of the group can become an MRP (Most Responsible Person) when a task needs to be completed or a resource gathered inside or outside the meeting. Every team member should be an MRP at one time or another. When everyone contributes, the work is balanced, and positive energy and goodwill spread.

The most effective teams are clear about the why, what, where, how, and when of their work. They are also clear about *who* is doing what. Defined roles and responsibilities may seem formal, and I have heard individuals say, "We do not like to get caught up with planning and process. We just want to work." As team leader, acknowledge this perspective, and explain that you have been using some of these tools and that you want to incorporate a few components in your meetings. Do not overwhelm team members with details; stay focused on student learning and the functions of collaborative teams. Use simple concepts and language that will fit your team. When the team sees results, members will appreciate its structure: "Our team is focused and organized. We share roles and responsibilities, and we get our work done."

3. Structure

The structure includes all the components one considers to create an effective team. It could be compared to building a home: If you do not have a blueprint, you will not have a plan to ensure that each room works with the structure as a whole. If you forget to build the foundation, the house will topple over. All the structural components must work together and be considered when you build an effective team.

Charts and Visuals

Visuals increase learning, group dynamics, attention, and ownership in your team. In *The Science of Non-Verbal Communication*, Michael Grinder (1997) teaches us that the visual communication tool allows the reader to process at his or her own rate and to look at the words as often has he or she needs to. The visual respects different types of learners. An oral presentation or statement can get lost, and participants may lose focus. The visual becomes the record; it makes the work of the team public. Recording and posting their words can also help individuals avoid "looping"—repeating the same idea or statements over and over.

Effective visuals help your team own the work and refocus when the conversation begins to stray. Participants see their words captured and know they are contributing. They also know they are being listened to and understood. Charts are powerful organizers and used well, become a structural tool for your team.

Every team needs an easel and chart in its meeting space to allow you to jump up at any time and capture the thinking and the agreements. Follow these simple rules for recording: Use white space, large printing, use earth-colored (blue, green, black, and brown) water-soluble markers, change colors for each idea or line, and record exactly what you hear. Deliberate use of color assists the participant in following the conversation; earth colors are easy on the eye and easy to read. Use red only to highlight or underline a point (Brandt, 1989). Clarify and honor the participation. If you are charting, make sure everyone's ideas are recorded.

Placement

Another strategy for creating positive structure is to move certain kinds of information off to the side (Grinder, 1997). If you are finished with one part of the meeting, for example, move the charts so they will not interfere with the next topic.

The "third point" technique is also helpful: If someone raises a sensitive issue, write it on the chart or a sheet of paper, and hold it off to the side. This separates difficult information from the sender and the receiver: It is much easier and less threatening to look for solutions and possibilities when the problem is depersonalized, when we are looking at a "third point" on paper rather than at a person in the room—especially when we are directly involved.

This technique is especially helpful when discussing assessment results. Post the results of student performance anonymously in a graph form, and ask the team to engage in a simple protocol. Tom Many asks teachers to use the "Here's What, So What? Now What?" method (Garmston & Wellman, 1999) for discussing the results of a common assessment. Once the overall results are posted, the team looks at the data in aggregate on the poster while privately comparing their own data to the group results.

Agenda

Most effective teams use a written agenda to keep the group focused and on track. The agenda is the road map to accomplish goals and purpose. Create the agenda after you know what you want to accomplish.

An agenda describes content and process. Start with the end in mind, and map backwards. What activities will get the team to the desired result and your session objectives? Your team might write down a title or a critical question for each agenda item, or your team may like longer agendas with more detail including time frames, decision points, and designation of who is responsible (MRP).

I like to post the purpose, agenda, and norms at each meeting on chart paper to introduce the work and check for agreement on the task at hand. Each team is different, and your process can vary within a team, too: You may not create charts each time you meet. The Team Organizer may be sufficient. The key is to find some way to show the team that you have a plan and direction. As the meeting progresses, you can even check off components. It is a subtle but helpful move to show progress.

Defining Norms

Norms are behavioral guidelines and agreements about how we will work together. Your team should have explicit norms that are created by and agreed upon by all the members of your team. Norms are intended to remind us about how we want to treat each other. They help us take risks, work through issues, and communicate well. They should be stated in the positive.

> **Our Science Team will:**
>
> - Start and end on time.
>
> - Ask, "Is this best for students?"
>
> - Listen respectfully, to understand first and respond second.
>
> - Balance participation and share airspace.
>
> - Pause, paraphrase, and probe for specificity.
>
> - Honor diverse perspectives and encourage participation.
>
> - Produce products and celebrate success.
>
> - Do the work in the meeting and not in the parking lot.
>
> - Respect confidentiality.
>
> - Agree to disagree while we are in the room.

To develop norms, see the processes shared by the National Staff Development Council and described in *Learning by Doing* (DuFour, DuFour, Eaker, & Many, 2006, pp. 210–212).

Sometimes we hear the comment, "My team is so dysfunctional. They don't trust each another." Remember that teams are comprised of individuals. We are each responsible for productivity and effective communication. As Garmston and Wellman point out, "There is no such thing as group behavior. All 'group behavior' results from the decisions and actions of individuals. When individual choices align in productive patterns, the group produces positive results" (1999, p. 33).

Your team norms will become especially important when you experience conflict. Instead of pointing fingers at individuals, it is helpful to call attention to norms. Placing the norms on the Team Organizer will prevent many negative behaviors. Evaluate your norms two or three times a year. To stay productive, bring attention to them often during regular meetings:

- Ask, "What is working, and what we need to work on at the end of the meeting?"

- Clarify norms before a difficult conversation. Ask team members to paraphrase norms before a difficult conversation and to describe what they see when the norm is being followed during the conversation.

- Ask, "What have we done in the past 3 weeks that demonstrates our commitment to the norms?"

- Brainstorm what each norm looks like and sounds like in meetings.

- Check in at the beginning of a meeting: Ask members, "Describe the norm that will be most important to pay attention to as we work today."

Preventative strategies are intentional. When you expect difficult conversations, spending 5 to 7 minutes to review norms first will pay off substantially.

Decision-Making Process

How will your team make decisions? What type of decision will you use? How will you know when a decision has been made?

The answers to these questions must be explicit and stated before a task. Your team may become confused if they think they are *deciding* something when in reality the team was supposed to be recommending. Recall and state out loud the type of decision you are involved in. Teach the following continuum of decisions to your team so you can use similar language and have shared understanding.

- **Autocratic**—One person will make the decision.

- **Consultative**—One person or one entity will make the decision after they have sought input.

- **Majority**—More than half of the participants agree with the proposal.

- **Near or sufficient consensus**—A predetermined number of participants agree with the proposal. Your team must decide what percentage feels like near consensus.

- **PLC consensus**—All points of view have been considered, and the will of the team is evident, even to those most opposed to it (DuFour, DuFour, Eaker, & Many, 2006).

Determine how you will demonstrate agreement. Some teams like to use thumbs up or down. It allows every person a visual representation and forces movement. If a team member has his thumb down, he talks about why and explains his concerns. The team can respectfully acknowledge the concerns and then state, "It is clear that the will of the group is to move forward, knowing there may be some concerns." The next step is for everyone to support and implement the decision.

Evaluation of Your Results and Team Time

The final structural and procedural component is checking to see that you are on track. Many teams use a formal survey once or twice a year to collect data and inform leadership. Teams may also use quick tools to check progress on an ongoing basis. Plan for time at the end of each meeting to summarize what you did, name the products created, clarify next meeting's task, and ask simple and quick checkout questions: "What worked for us today?" "What do we need to focus on or do differently next meeting?" Keep changing how you ask, but do not hesitate to ask. Checking shows you care and that you want your team time to be valuable and productive.

4. Process

Process is the method of conducting meetings and engaging participants. It is a series of actions that move teams closer to their goals.

Members will engage and follow a process if they think it will help accomplish the task. They will disengage if they think it is unrelated and too time-intensive. Process must match intended objectives and help you accomplish your goals. Be deliberate and focused on results when determining what process will work best for you.

Grounding and Check

Bob Chadwick (2000), friend and mentor from Terrebonne, Oregon, reminds us that we all have a need to be part of a community. We are not isolated creatures by preference. If we feel connected to each other, we will be more motivated to work together and spend time together.

Begin your meetings with the focus and purpose comments, and then move to a check-in or grounding. We call this step *grounding* because it brings us to the here and now; it establishes our place in the team, and it balances power. We all participate from the very beginning.

Always ask each person: "Please share your name, your expectations for today, and how you feel about being here." Some team leaders like to bypass the last part—"how you feel"—for fear that a teammate might express negative comments. That can happen, but at least then the feelings are public and explicit. It is hard to deal with "under the table" issues.

Ownership and a sense of accountability occur when each person checks in. Over time, teammates will become open during grounding and express real fears and hopes. Grounding establishes a model and a tone for deep listening. Every person will have a voice and be heard, and each person will establish verbal territory. The facilitator or leader will not be doing all the work.

Protocols and Tools

Protocols force transparency by segmenting elements of a conversation whose boundaries otherwise blur: talking and listening, describing and judging, proposing and giving feedback.

—James McDonald et al.

Complex systems such as collaborative teams need collective commitments to be productive. Your team will be more honest and achieve more clarity when members do not worry about "stepping on" each other or become confused about how to participate. Protocols provide consistent structure to conversations and create a sense of safety around expressing opinions. They invite deep thinking and reflection, allowing team members to say what is truly on their minds. The steps will slow the conversation down and stop others from interrupting before their turn. Each team member knows he or she will have an opportunity to speak, thus members stop their inner self-talk and listen to each other more. In other words, protocols "constrain participation in order to heighten it" (McDonald et al., 2007, p. ix).

When choosing protocols, always consider balance. Ask yourself, "How is the process engaging everyone on our team to accomplish our goal?" Remember, your team members have diverse styles of learning. Members are introverts and extroverts with a variety of needs and desires. Be bold! Try different strategies in your team meetings. Observe which protocols served your purpose and helped your team become more productive. Think about all the different instructional strategies you use in your classroom. Many of these work in adult groups, too. Examples include the following:

- **Think, pair, share**—Asking team members to reflect and write about the topic or issue, then partner and share their thoughts

- **Go-round**—Creating a circle and then allowing each person to share to share his or her thoughts in turn

- **Text or "jigsaw"**—Asking each team member to read a section of article or text from a book, summarize key points, meet with an "expert" group to discuss the key points, and then teach the segment to the team or whole group

- **Force-field analysis**—Listing, as a group, the forces restraining and supporting a current situation's improvement

Be intentional with the process and protocols. Be a connoisseur who collects them. Use them to accomplish your goals while at the same time building community.

5. Behaviors and Relationships

As a teacher and then as principal, I learned over and over again that the relationship among adults in the schoolhouse has more impact on the quality and character of the school—and on the accomplishment of youngsters—than any other factor.

—Roland Barth

Individuals want to be connected. We tend to feel a sense of belonging with those we work with. We desire respect from our colleagues and want to be accepted and included in key decisions. Paying attention to the five components of effective collaboration and using the suggestions described in this chapter will provide opportunities for your team to engage in heart-to-heart conversations and break through to more authentic relationships.

But in addition, you must take responsibility for your own interpersonal skills. Communication is like teaching, both an art and a science. Working with our peers can be challenging, especially when we find ourselves with little time and exponential student needs. So practice what works. Attend to both verbal and nonverbal communication. Refer to the following communications tips when you need a refresher or you are finding yourself struggling.

Nonverbal Communication Techniques

- **Listen**—Bend your ears around what the person speaking is saying. Listen to understand first and respond second. Nod, provide eye contact, and show respect by allowing the person to complete his or her thoughts.

- **Pause**—Do not jump into the empty space in a conversation. Allow the speaker 3 to 5 seconds to gather thoughts and provide more detail. Wait until others have contributed.

- **Adjust your voice**—Your tone, inflections, rate, and volume all matter. Use the credible voice to make a point and call for attention. Use the approachable voice to pique interest and involvement. Michael Grinder (1997) describes that our voice patterns will fall somewhere on a continuum between credibility on one end and approachability on the other. The credible voice pattern is used to send information and increase importance. It is characterized by more pauses, intonations that curl down at the end of a statement or word, and the speaker's head holding still when as she delivers the message. The approachable voice includes more head nodding, more rhythmic patterns, and intonations that curl up on the end of a statement or word. Notice what happens when you are conscious of your voice in your team meetings.

- **Adjust your stance and breathing**—Use the frozen gesture (Grinder, 1997) in combination with a pause to hold a listener's attention. Hold your hand waist high or above the table as a way to pace the conversation. Team members won't consciously focus on your hand movement, but they will react to the pause plus a gesture signaling them to wait and let another finish. The frozen gesture can also be used to make a point, pause, and hold the attention of the listener. In addition, your stance and where you place yourself in the group will convey meaning to others. If you stand and talk a lot, it signals "I have the power" and will do the work. Think about how you sit in relation to your teammates, and balance power by sitting around a circle. When your team hits a snag or disagrees, let all team members voice their point of view; accept the increased volume, passion, and pace of the conversation. If necessary, you can deliberately slow the pace down and help others be resourceful by taking a few deep breaths. This will restore balance, activate higher order thinking, regulate blood flow, and demonstrate that all is well. Our breathing can regulate the energy in the room. Take deep breaths, and notice how you and others around you relax.

Verbal Techniques

- **Reframing**—Turn negative statements or perceptions into positives. It is best to do it without certainty. Example: "He is so stubborn!" Reply: "It seems to me that stubbornness may be a quality of independence and strong conviction. How do those qualities provide value to our team?"

- **Checking perceptions**—Do not jump to conclusions or make assumptions without checking out your perceptions: "Let me check this out. I am thinking this is the will of the group. Am I correct?"

- **Paraphrasing**—Restate what you hear and honor the speaker. Paraphrase to seek agreement, clarify content, summarize, and shift the level of abstraction. Garmston and Wellman (1999) remind us, "Paraphrasing is one of the most valuable and least used communication tools in meetings. . . . Groups that develop consciousness about paraphrasing and give themselves permission to use this reflected tool become clearer and more cohesive about their work" (pp. 39–40). Be as natural as possible when paraphrasing and practice. Examples include: "So you are thinking . . ." "You are suggesting that . . ." "You are concerned about . . ." "You seem to have two objectives; the first one is . . ." Notice that paraphrases are not questions, but statements that allow others to feel heard and respected.

- **Articulating your point of view**—Tell your truth. Describe what you see from your vantage point, and make clear, actionable requests or statements (Sparks, 2005). Stay away from "but" at the beginning of a sentence. Instead, use: "And, this is another way to think about it . . ." or "My perspective is . . ."

Working Together Effectively

Interpersonal and communication skills combined with the other four elements—focus, roles and responsibilities, structure, and process—do make a difference in your team's results. Decide now that positive and productive meetings are the norm and a standard for your team. Influence through your behaviors and your actions. Keep a relentless focus on student learning, and remember that no amount of reading, contemplating, and talking will substitute for *doing*. Do not hesitate; do something and begin. Take initiative and introduce the content formally to your team, or bring in the ideas through your daily actions. You can improve the quality of your relationships, your interactions, and most importantly, the student learning in your school through your daily leadership.

References

Barth, R. (2001). *Learning by heart.* San Francisco: Jossey-Bass.

Bossidy, L., & Charan, R. (2002). *Execution: The discipline of getting things done.* New York: Crown Business.

Brandt, R. (1989). *Flip charts: How to draw them and how to use them.* San Francisco: Jossey-Bass/Pfeiffer.

Centennial BOCES. (2002). *Standards-based classroom operator's manual.* Alexandria, VA: Just Ask Publications.

Chadwick, R. (2000). *Colorado Educators Consensus Institute: Beyond conflict to consensus.* Terrebonne, OR: Consensus Associates.

DuFour, R., DuFour, R., Eaker, R., & Many, T. (2006). *Learning by doing: A handbook for professional learning communities at work*. Bloomington, IN: Solution Tree.

Fullan, M., & Germain, C. (2006). *Learning places: A field guide for improving the context of schooling*. Thousand Oaks, CA: Corwin.

Garmston, R., & Wellman, B. (1999). *The adaptive school: A sourcebook for developing collaborative groups*. Norwood, MA: Christopher-Gordon.

Grinder, M. (1997). *The science of non-verbal communication*. St. Battle Ground, WA: Author.

McDonald, J., Mohr, N., Dichter, A., & McDonald, E. (2007). *The power of protocols: An educator's guide to better practice*. New York: Teachers College.

Schmoker, M. (2006). *Results now: How we can achieve unprecedented improvements in teaching and learning*. Alexandria, VA: Association for Supervision and Curriculum Development.

Sparks, D. (2005). *Leading for results: Transforming teaching, learning, and relationships in schools*. Thousand Oaks, CA: Corwin; National Staff Development Council.

THOMAS W. MANY

 As superintendent of Kildeer Countryside Community Consolidated School District 96 in Buffalo Grove, Illinois, Tom Many keeps a sharp focus on school improvement issues. He uses the tenets of Professional Learning Communities at Work™ to ensure students from his district are prepared to enter Adlai Stevenson High School, a model PLC. In each of his roles—superintendent, public speaker, and author—he has worked closely with Dr. Rick DuFour, former superintendent of Stevenson and national authority on how to transform schools into professional learning communities. Tom's long and distinguished career includes 17 years experience as superintendent. He has also served as a classroom teacher, learning center director, curriculum supervisor, principal, and assistant superintendent. A dedicated PLC practitioner, he has been involved in local- and state-level initiatives to achieve school improvement. Under his direction, District 96 has been recognized as one of the highest achieving and lowest spending elementary districts in Illinois.

THREE

Teacher Talk:
How Collaboration Gets to the
Heart of Great Schools

Thomas W. Many

Members of a professional learning community recognize they cannot accomplish their fundamental purpose of high levels of learning for all students unless they work together collaboratively.

—Richard DuFour, Rebecca DuFour,
Robert Eaker, & Thomas Many

Much has been written on the need to collaborate, the benefits of collaborating, and the process of collaboration. We know that when teachers work together to improve their professional practice, student learning improves. Why is collaboration at the heart of what makes schools better?

Those most effective in meeting the learning needs of their students will create collaborative cultures in which educators pool their knowledge, effort, and energy to learn from one another. Indeed, Michael Fullan sees the creation of collaborative cultures as essential to making progress. He notes, "Without the collaborative skills and relationships, it is not possible to learn and to continue to learn as much as you [teachers] need to know" to improve schools (Fullan, 1993, pp. 17–18).

Breaking With Tradition

The kind of collaborative culture envisioned by Fullan is in stark contrast with the environment of a traditional school where teachers work in isolation with little time to share ideas or reflect on their practice, where school goals are the responsibility of the principal, and where the voice heard at the faculty meeting is often that of the teacher with the longest tenure. These traditions create a powerful barrier to the kind of environment that is most conducive to collaboration—a professional learning community in which educators are committed to working together to help their students achieve better results.

Having worked with teachers in 32 states and three provinces of Canada, I've observed that those who collaborate effectively with their colleagues—those who make collaboration count—made changes in three areas: practice, language, and relationships. Wanting to better understand the nature of the changes and how they came about, I asked teachers and principals to respond to a simple three-part question: "As your school becomes more collaborative, what has changed in terms of practice, language, and relationships?" I was curious; exactly what is it that needs to be done? What kinds of changes must occur to move teachers from time-honored patterns of working in isolation to working in collaborative cultures that more effectively serve students?

Over 18 months in 2006 and 2007, I forwarded an informal survey to principals and teacher leaders from around the United States and received dozens of responses from educators in Alabama, Colorado, Illinois, Louisiana, Minnesota, and Wisconsin. Their answers reflected a passionate desire to create the kinds of collaborative cultures that help all students succeed.

Respondents to the email survey reported the biggest change since becoming a PLC was the increase in the amount of *time and effort* they spend collaborating. They pointed to two specific factors that fostered this change: 1) a schedule that allows more time for collaboration during the regular school day, and 2) the principal's expectation that teachers will work together.

If a schedule that allows teachers to collaborate is important, then creating protected, dedicated time for collaboration during the regular school day is essential. As an instructional coach in Littleton, Colorado, reported, "We have altered our school day to include common planning times for grade-level departments and our staff meetings are now focused on PLC business." There is never enough time for everything, but creating time for collaboration during the teachers' regular school day sends a strong message about what is important.

Another teacher observed that after the schedule at her school was rearranged to reflect a higher priority on formal opportunities for collaboration, teachers began to take advantage of informal opportunities to share ideas: "We have begun to collaborate on important topics in the teachers' lounge, on the sidewalk, before and after school, through emails and phone calls. [We] are more focused on how to improve the students' work environment and much less on complaining" (high school teacher, Grant, Louisiana). It seems simple, but schools that are creating more collaborative cultures have made the *conscious* choice to find the time for collaboration during the teachers' regular school day.

No question, changing a school's culture from one of isolation to collaboration is a significant shift, but in schools working to become a PLC, "you can't get away with total isolation anymore" (middle school teacher, Longmont, Colorado). An elementary classroom teacher in Longmont noted changes as well: "There are more teams putting greater effort into working together rather than in isolation."

To be successful, an Elk Grove, Illinois, teacher argued, teachers need to be given *time* to reflect upon the rationale behind this shift: "The more people I have to collaborate with, the more expertise that I can pool, and the greater amount of time I have to think critically, out of the box, about kids, [the more I know] about my students, instruction, and assessment."

Dylan Wiliam observed, "Teacher learning communities appear to be the most effective, practical method for changing day to day classroom practice" (2007/2008, p. 39), but when every minute of a teaching day is scheduled in classrooms or in supervising students, teachers don't get the quantity or quality of time they need to talk about their practice with colleagues. In order to respond to the challenge of changing their practice, teachers need an opportunity to collaborate.

Consider what is required of an experienced teacher being asked to make the shift from a focus on teaching to a focus on learning—one of the big ideas of a professional learning community. Many veteran teachers were trained with an intense concentration on improving lesson design and delivery, in accordance with Madeline Hunter's seven-step lesson design. Their training was directed toward teaching and how to improve it.

So, when we suggest that the focus should shift from teaching to learning—from whether a teacher taught a solid lesson to whether students learned it—veterans might ask, "Whatever happened to setting clear objectives, creating an anticipatory set, and providing opportunities for guided practice?" In veteran teachers' experience, even a conversation around checking for understanding has always centered on "Did I check for understanding?" But the question now being asked is not whether the teacher checked for understanding but rather, "What will I do if students did or didn't understand?"

Responses to the email survey indicate that, given time to collaborate, teachers in professional learning communities embrace the opportunity to discuss their practice. As one elementary teacher from Schaumburg, Illinois, explained, "My favorite part of working [here] is the professional conversations that happen. They are interesting, informative, essential, and sometimes heated. However, they are at the heart of what makes our instruction successful."

When asked what had changed as a result of more collaboration, a high school teacher in Grant, Louisiana, reported, "It would be easier to answer what has *not* changed! The school works to make sure all students achieve success. We collaborate more with each other as teachers, with the administration, and with the parents. Our test scores are very high and I attribute it [improved levels of student achievement] to this collaboration."

Just as importantly, successful schools identify what practices teams should focus on during team meetings. Simply giving teachers time to work together in teams will not guarantee school improvement. Indeed, "the pertinent question is not, 'Are teachers collaborating?' but rather, 'What are teachers collaborating about?'" (DuFour, DuFour, Eaker, & Many, 2006, p. 91). The experience of teachers in District 54, a No Child Left Behind 2007 Blue Ribbon Award-winning school district in Schaumburg, Illinois, has led the superintendent to comment, "It is clear that we can no longer pretend we don't know what practices improve student learning. [District 54] teachers have never been more focused or clear on what needs to be done."

How Is Collaboration Changing Practice?

A focus on changing a few specific, high-leverage practices yields great results. Teachers and principals who responded to the email survey reported that specific changes in their practice began with 1) examining the essential outcomes that teachers expect students to know and be able to do at the end of a class, course, or grade level;

then moved to 2) using data to give them information about student progress; and included 3) developing systematic ways to respond to students who did and did not learn what was expected. The alignment of curriculum and instruction, the use of data to drive instructional decisions, and the attention to interventions are big changes that have a positive and measurable effect.

Aligning Curriculum and Instruction

A significant change in practice identified by teachers and principals was the alignment of the curriculum and articulation around essential outcomes: "My teachers talk about learning targets, what is essential, and what is nice to know" (middle school principal, Loveland, Colorado).

A simple strategy some teachers are using to foster both collaboration and curriculum alignment is known as Keep, Drop, and Create. At least once a grading period, teachers bring their lesson plan books and copies of their school's essential curriculum to a meeting of peers. They post three pieces of butcher paper on the meeting room wall and label the first sheet *Keep,* the second *Drop,* and the third *Create.* Each teacher is given sticky notes in three colors—yellow for Keep, pink for Drop, and green for Create. Meeting by grade level or in departmental teams, they begin the process of analyzing and reflecting on their teaching together.

Using their plan books as the record of what was taught (the implemented curriculum) and copies of their school's essential curriculum (the prescribed curriculum), the teachers compare one subject at a time and begin categorizing the topics they taught during the previous grading period into one of the Keep, Drop, or Create categories.

Topics reflected as part of the essential curriculum *and* included in the teachers' lesson plan books are written on the yellow sticky notes and placed in the Keep column. Topics reflected as part of the essential curriculum but *not* included in the teachers' lesson plan books—because they haven't been taught yet or were skipped—are captured on green sticky notes and then placed in the Create column. Finally, those topics included in a teacher's lesson plan book but *not* reflected as part of the essential curriculum are noted on pink sticky notes and posted in the Drop column.

As each topic is identified, noted on a sticky note, and captured on the butcher paper, a list of topics for the grading period emerges. Teachers check the topics captured within the Keep and Create categories and then match those topics with four to five corresponding questions on the most recent common assessment. Regular use of this activity helps them identify nonessential curriculum—those topics listed on the Drop page—and helps create a "Stop Doing" list.

In addition to creating a framework for the development of common assessments, the feedback generated by the Keep, Drop, Create activity helps teachers focus their planning, pace their instruction, and align the essential curriculum with the intended curriculum. An elementary principal in Buffalo Grove, Illinois, proudly noted, "Our teachers know that we do not have to be on the exact same page as we present our instruction, but we do know we have to be similar in our expectations and pacing of materials."

Using Data to Drive Instructional Decisions

Another change highlighted by teachers in the email survey was the increased use of data. According to an elementary teacher in Littleton, Colorado, "We use data to support our goals, to direct our teaching, and to determine when we have reached those goals." Teachers in these schools use results of formative assessments to provide information on student progress; their conversations shift from process to outcomes and from a focus on instruction to a focus on what students actually learn: "The 'teacherspeak' [in our school] has changed from 'I think' to 'I know' that's how he performed on the test" (special education teacher, Colorado Springs, Colorado).

In order to use collaboration time efficiently, teachers are adopting protocols for analyzing data. One strategy that teams have found helpful is to apply the Here's What, So What? Now What? protocol during the course of a 30-minute team meeting.

By looking at the data and making factual statements about what the data says, the teachers define "Here's What" in the first 5 minutes of a meeting. For example, they determine the Here's What by using the results of an assessment to look for patterns of strengths and weaknesses, paying attention to the topic areas in which students scored the highest and lowest, the schools or classes that scored the highest and lowest, and the particular item(s) that most students answered incorrectly.

The teachers then take the next 10 minutes to discuss the implications of the data—the "So What?" They write fact statements to describe the problem; for example, they note that sixth graders are misunderstanding the correct use of quotation marks. They hypothesize reasons for the students' lack of clarity and accept or reject the reason(s) suggested, then determine the top two areas of greatest need shown by the data.

This schedule leaves the final 15 minutes of the meeting to be devoted to planning what to do next—the "Now What?" step. At this point, the teachers plan specific actions to address the two areas of greatest need, such as including more homework items with sentences that require students to apply their understanding of using quotation marks.

The Here's What, So What? Now What? three-step protocol is an efficient and effective strategy that helps teams analyze data quickly and meaningfully. The "just-in-time" knowledge that teachers acquire about student progress allows them to target specific strategies for improving student learning. As a fine arts teacher in Littleton, Colorado, observed, "I am more attuned to the weekly (sometimes daily) achievement levels of my students. I make adjustments to my daily teaching based on these results."

Developing Interventions

A third high-leverage practice teachers reported in the survey is the creation of systematic intervention strategies. Teachers across the country are retooling their daily schedules to find time for students who need extra support in their learning. These schools are committed to doing whatever it takes to create opportunities for more time and support during the regular school day.

Teachers in Twin Groves and Woodlawn Middle Schools in Chicago's northwest suburbs have rearranged a traditional middle school schedule to allow early afternoon academic intervention periods every Wednesday and Thursday. Two days a week, 4 minutes are shaved off the end of each class period and "collected" to create a 30-minute Academic Extension period right after lunch. The entire school follows the normal schedule 3 days a week and the alternate schedule 2 days a week. By shortening the standard schedule by a few minutes per period, extra time is created without impacting the regular routine of the school.

During these 30-minute Academic Extension periods, students go for reteaching of a concept in a particular discipline, visit the computer lab or Learning Center to do research for a project, or attend a study hall where teachers offer homework assistance. "The one-on-one attention that students get during the intervention [Academic Extension] time has helped immeasurably," one teacher from Buffalo Grove reported. "Students learn material that was difficult for them, but more importantly it helps their confidence. Students who were quiet, hiding behind their hair, or slumped in their desks are suddenly actively participating and engaged."

Using this approach, the services of *all* the teachers are available to *all* the students—every teacher and aide in the building is a part of the in-school intervention program and all of the children are served by it. As another Buffalo Grove teacher observed, "Interventions [Academic Extension] are a great way to get to know students on a one-on-one basis. While you [the teacher] are honing in on their particular strengths and weaknesses, students are able to ask questions in a small setting which truly allows for personal growth and understanding." She continued, "The greatest part for me, the teacher, is that I am able to see immediate changes in the students to help them in classroom instruction and overall comprehension on a particular topic."

The faculty at Link Elementary School in Elk Grove, Illinois, has adopted a unique way to generate intervention time during their day. By working together to agree on pacing of the curriculum, teachers use flexible grouping as an effective way to provide more time and support to students.

The pacing of the core curriculum is carefully planned. Each team develops an instructional calendar and a corresponding formative assessment that is given to students on a regular basis. Teachers meet to review the results and regroup the students based on the assessment results. Based upon the assessment results, students receive instruction on the following day with different teachers, where they engage in relevant extension, enrichment, or remedial activities.

The intervention plan at Link Elementary School requires a high level of collaboration, but teachers find a way to provide ongoing time and support without disrupting the normal school routine. By providing more frequent in-school intervention opportunities, they ensure that students do not "slip through the cracks" and that those struggling with a concept or missing homework assignments do not fall behind.

How Is Collaboration Changing Language?

As teachers collaborate, their focus on changing their practices highlights a change in the language of their school. In focused conversations, they discover 1) the need for greater clarity around new terminology and 2) the need to agree on the implications of the terminology.

Indeed, clarity around language is essential, and achieving it requires conversation. A memo or an announcement won't suffice to transmit meaning. For teachers to understand the meaning and implications of the language of collaboration, they must participate in the process of creating shared understanding. To paraphrase Kouzes and Posner (2002), the language of collaboration is "forged, not forced."

The Need for Greater Clarity

In the schools I surveyed, specific changes in teachers' practice led to significant changes in their language. A middle school principal in Sheridan, Colorado, said, "I've overheard conversations in which teachers are using the data to explain growth. *Data* and *results* were not in our vocabulary 4 years ago." For a professional learning community to exist, teachers must talk and reach consensus on the terms and the meanings that comprise the language of their practice.

Using activities ranging from simple BINGO games to sophisticated mental models designed to reinforce vocabulary, teachers across North America have been engaged in conversation with their colleagues to clarify and create a shared understanding of seemingly commonplace words. In a PLC, being "confused" about the meaning of important vocabulary—often a subtle and politically correct form of resistance—is not tolerated.

In one school, teachers developed a whole new understanding of the terrible "–tions": terms such as *evaluation, differentiation, remediation, accommodation,* and *intervention.* Teachers used Venn diagrams to compare and contrast the similarities and differences of *remediation* and *intervention*. After discussing these terms, teachers developed key characteristics to use when deciding whether an idea would more appropriately be described as one or the other.

In addressing how collaboration has changed their language, teachers in the survey reported that they and their fellow staff members have devoted considerable time to clarifying terminology. Teams worked to identify and then define key vocabulary such as *summative* and *formative assessment* or *intervention* and *remediation*. In fact, they reported they often spent entire faculty meetings discussing and defining the language of a PLC!

Agreeing on the Implications

Teachers also reported spending time discussing the implications of important terminology. For example, what is the difference between a power standard (essential outcome) and a supporting standard? Could the same test be *both* summative and formative? Could a child participate in short-term interventions and still be eligible for long-term remedial or special education programs?

Michael Fullan wrote, "The terms of reform—*professional learning community, capacity building, assessment for learning*—travel easily, but the underlying conceptualization does not. Think of . . . an iceberg, the vast majority of which is underwater. Many leaders take shortcuts by slicing off the visible part of the iceberg and then assuming that they have captured its full power" (Fullan, Bertani, & Quinn, 2004, p. 42).

We spend far too little time in schools developing a common understanding of the language of collaboration. Teachers must not only agree on the specific terminology to describe new and evolving practice, they must also agree on the *implications* of the new terminology. In other words, they must work together to co-create meaning around the big ideas of a professional learning community.

This was made clear to me when I was confronted by a music teacher who was less than enamored with making the change she saw a professional learning community requiring of her. "I'm sick and tired of 'PLC this' and 'PLC that,'" she said, confronting me in the hallway of her school. "If you take the 'L' out of PLC," she told me, "all you have left is 'PC.' I have never been politically correct before, and I am not going to start now!"

After stopping for a moment—mostly to allow us both to gather ourselves—I realized she was frustrated, and I could appreciate her confusion. It seems that educators everywhere are calling anything and everything PLC. I've heard districts describe how their PLC teams meet on "PLC Days"—as if these teams were uniquely configured to accomplish all their work on the second and fourth Tuesdays of the month.

Returning to my experience with the music teacher, I tried to gain some insight into her frustration by asking a series of questions: Did she believe there were certain aspects of the music curriculum that all her students should learn and be able to do? Did she believe knowing how her students were doing was critical to being a successful music teacher? Did she believe all kids could learn to appreciate music if given enough time and support? She answered with an emphatic, "Yes, of course. All of that is important!"

Clearly, this music teacher already understood effective teaching practices and was passionate about helping her students learn. She also understood the underlying meaning around some of the most important ideas of the professional learning community model. She knew good teaching even if she could not relate to the PLC terms we were using that day. The missing piece was the connection between what she intuitively knew as good teaching and the terminology of a PLC.

Teachers in the survey recognized that the changes brought by collaboration extended from their practice to their language; working together, they reached agreement on which terms were important and what they meant. In collaborative cultures, teachers engage in conversations that are more frequent and focused to co-create meaning around the big ideas of a professional learning community—and they do it together.

How Is Collaboration Changing Relationships?

A third major change survey respondents noted is the evolution of their relationships. Teachers and principals said that as the practice and language of a school changed, eventually, so did the relationships between and among the faculty and staff. Three facets of relationships changed: The educators developed a sense of 1) *shared responsibility* for the success of all students, 2) *mutual accountability* between and among faculty and staff, and 3) *reciprocal accountability* between teachers and administrators.

Shared Responsibility

It's noteworthy that teachers who once may have appreciated the anonymity that working in isolation offered them have come to welcome the shared responsibility for student success that is the foundation of professional learning communities. As one teacher in Elk Grove reported, "You no longer become a classroom teacher, or a fourth-grade teacher, but a building teacher. You [teachers] take ownership of learning for all students in the building."

The sense of having shared responsibility for students' learning is widespread and motivating. The changing relationships not only affect students in positive ways, but also teachers. Good teachers get even better as they benefit from collaborative relationships: "I have taken ideas from colleagues and implemented them in my classroom. I have been able to see another colleague has a better way of teaching and use that to help my students improve. It's collaboration, not competition" (middle school teacher, Elk Grove).

As teachers build more trust, they capitalize on this openness and learn from one another: "First we needed to learn to trust each other, separate the personal and professional conflict, and find a hint of success to continue to challenge each other. Now we've spread that to collaborating with other grade levels in our building. Whether we are sharing ideas, modeling instruction that works for us, or talking about kids that will one day be sixth graders, we are all determined, more than ever, to show everyone in our building how unstoppable and powerful we can all be" (elementary classroom teacher, Elk Grove).

Mutual Accountability

Survey respondents working in a PLC also reported higher levels of mutual accountability. The idea that teachers share responsibility for all students' learning—not just their own students' learning—has a significant and positive effect on teams. A middle school teacher in Grand Junction, Colorado, asserted, "The Administration asks us to commit to weekly [grade-level] meetings, but we decide on the goals, the outcomes, and what we want to accomplish." Given direction, teachers hold each other accountable for completing the work.

The superintendent of an elementary school in Schaumburg, Illinois, observed a similar trend in his schools: "I am seeing increased collaboration, increased accountability, increased focus on student learning." He continued, " I believe this is a result of [teachers] collaborating on a regular basis and holding each other accountable."

Teachers also reported satisfying results of this heightened sense of mutual accountability around working in teams. A special education teacher in Colorado Springs noted, "Our second grade team never worked as a team before. They are all strong teachers, but very individual. They have learned to do some compromising and now meet as a team two times a week, once to touch base and do general grade-level planning and once to talk about successes and needed changes."

Reciprocal Accountability

Beyond the commitment of teacher-to-teacher accountability, another facet of relationships changes with regard to responsibility. More collaborative relationships create the need for a heightened sense of shared responsibility between teachers and administrators. Elmore (2002) referred to this concept as *reciprocal accountability,* saying that "for every increment of performance I demand from you, I have an equal responsibility to provide you with the capacity to meet that expectation. Likewise, for every investment you make in my skill and knowledge, I have a reciprocal responsibility to demonstrate some new increment of performance" (p. 5). The concept of reciprocal accountability illustrates the importance of administrators accepting the responsibility to ensure that an expectation for improved student learning brings with it the requisite commitment to provide the necessary resources and collaborative time for staff.

When principals ask teachers to use data to drive instructional decisions, they recognize they have a responsibility to find the time for teachers to do their work. If principals ask teachers to assume an additional duty as part of an intervention, they recognize their responsibility to secure funds for a stipend. Without the presence of Elmore's principle of reciprocal responsibility—that is, without the principal's willingness to provide sufficient time and resources during the school day to collaborate and address students' needs through aligning of the curriculum, writing common assessments, and planning effective interventions—teachers lack what they need to bring about academic improvement for students.

As one elementary principal in Loveland, Colorado, said, "In the teams experiencing high levels of success with students . . . there is a higher level of job satisfaction [and] a higher level of efficacy among the teachers. I just give them room and support as they need it." In a professional learning community, teachers recognize the importance of their roles and principals accept the responsibility to do whatever it takes to make it possible for teachers to succeed.

Changes in Practice, Language, and Relationships Are Linked

In the process of creating more collaborative cultures, changes in practice link to changes in language that link to changes in relationships. The changes in practice—the increase in collaboration and the attention to specific, high-leverage behaviors—are observable. New practice prompts teachers to change the language in their schools as they work to clarify terminology and understand the implications of changing practice. Ultimately, changes in teachers' practice and language lead to changes in relationships that occur deep within the culture of a school.

The collaborative culture of a professional learning community creates a powerful commitment to best practice. An instructional coach in Elk Grove described it as follows: "A PLC is a noncompetitive environment that is not about who is the best teacher, but about how we can all be the best for our kids. . . . All teachers come into the profession thinking that we know a lot. But, what we do not know is how much we can learn from others. Working [collaboratively] as a PLC makes your school and your grade level stronger."

The collaborative culture of a professional learning community is a powerful motivation for learning linked to language. The need to clarify and co-create meaning sparks inquiry and generates momentum: "It's invigorating to come to work every day knowing we are going to have passionate conversations about our teaching and our students . . . to leave a meeting with other staff members ready to try something new and with a sense of 'what we're doing is best for kids'" (elementary classroom teacher, Elk Grove).

The collaborative culture of a professional learning community builds on the relationships of everyone at the school and simultaneously creates a sense of shared responsibility and mutual accountability. Two high school teachers in Grant, Louisiana, offered similar assessments of the change: "Teachers are no longer isolated and trying to solve problems alone. We have realized that we can bring our challenges to a group of fellow teachers and work out a solution together"; "Gone are the days of 'I teach/you teach.' Now WE teach all students, no matter the subject matter."

The collaborative cultures that are so fundamental to professional learning communities are at the heart of great schools. The principal of the high school in Grant concurred with the assessment of its teachers: "The entire culture of our school is different. Teachers taught in isolation, taught the curriculum—mostly just the textbook—and accepted mediocrity. Now, teachers collaborate and know what each other is teaching and how they are teaching. Now, instead of covering the curriculum, they teach students."

And when the links of practice, language, and relationships connect around learning, the kind of cultural shifts we need can occur, with positive results for student learning and for teachers invested in their work. A 25-year veteran teacher in Loveland said, "I haven't had this much fun teaching in years! . . . My head spins when we talk about student work, but that's part of it. I understand the complexity of what I do and I feel empowered by the fact that . . . it directly impacts students in a positive way." At the heart of a great school, a collaborative culture reawakens a teacher's sense of purpose. A middle school teacher in Elk Grove summed up the feelings of many teachers in the survey: "I would never want to be the only person that knows the students in my classroom. Our students are receiving a better education due to the hard work and dedication of all the adults that are here to work for kids, with kids, and because of kids."

References

DuFour, R., DuFour, R., Eaker, R., & Many, T. (2006). *Learning by doing: A handbook for professional learning communities at work*. Bloomington, IN: Solution Tree.

Elmore, R. (2002). *Bridging the gap between standards and achievement: The imperative for professional development in education*. Washington, DC: The Albert Shanker Institute.

Fullan, M. (1993). *Change forces: Probing the depths of educational reform*. London: The Falmer Press.

Fullan, M., Bertani, A., & Quinn, J. (2004). New lessons for districtwide reform. *Educational Leadership, 61*(7), 42–46.

Kouzes, J., & Posner, B. (2002). *The leadership challenge* (3rd ed.). San Francisco: Jossey-Bass.

Wiliam, D. (December 2007/January 2008). Changing classroom practice. *Educational Leadership, 65*(4), 36–42.

Part Two

CREATING A GUARANTEED AND VIABLE CURRICULUM

CHRIS JAKICIC

Chris Jakicic, Ed.D., served as principal of Woodlawn Middle School in Long Grove, Illinois, from its opening day in 1999 through the spring of 2007. Under her leadership, the staff shifted toward a collaborative culture focused on learning, and they implemented assessment *for* learning practices to shape their instructional strategies. Their efforts have made a difference in student success levels. Ever since the teachers began collaborating to write common assessments, engaging students in self-assessment, and making grades more transparent, student motivation and performance have increased. In addition, Woodlawn is one of the schools featured as evidence of effectiveness on the professional learning communities website, www.allthingsplc.info.

FOUR

Too Much to Teach:
How to Identify What Matters Most

Chris Jakicic

You have a curriculum guide, a textbook, a teacher's guide, and a copy of your state standards, but do you really know what you're expected to teach? Even teachers with a great deal of experience have a difficult time choosing from among all of the possible curricula written for their grade level or subject area. For new teachers it's even more difficult to distinguish merely important content from *essential* content.

Many states have 50 to 60 performance descriptors or grade-level expectations for each subject area for teachers to use as they plan their curriculum. Teachers must review these expectations, determine how to sequence them, decide how much time to spend teaching them, and establish criteria for what mastery of the standard looks like. Even with a teacher-developed curriculum guide, teachers are making dozens of decisions about curriculum each time they write lesson plans.

What results is what Schmoker and Marzano (1999) call curriculum chaos. They suggest that we have two or three times more than what we realistically can teach. Because this requires individual teachers to make individual decisions, they argue, "such practices create huge holes in the continuum of content to which students are exposed." What if a school were to rely on the standards published by each subject area's national organization? Marzano and Kendall

(1998) looked at these standards and the amount of time normally allocated in the school day for instruction. They subsequently calculated that students would need to attend school for *22 years* if all of the published standards were to be adequately covered.

Why Essential Outcomes Matter

Consider the following scenario in a school whose teachers worked to carefully describe exactly what is expected from student writing in each genre at each grade level. Middle school teachers at Woodlawn Middle School in Long Grove, Illinois, chose a schoolwide focus on writing after determining that this was the content area of greatest need for their students. After 3 full years working to develop and implement an agreed-upon set of essential outcomes and assessments for writing, Woodlawn teachers began to see student writing improving. Teachers became much more convinced that they knew what is expected from students at each grade level. At the beginning of the 2006–2007 school year, eighth-grade language arts teachers reported that for the first time ever, all students in their classes scored at "meeting standards" in their first common assessment of the year in writing. While this achievement took time and required teachers of all subject areas to support the process, the final outcome was worth all their hard work, according to these teachers.

Why is this story important? When teacher teams work together to answer the first critical question of a professional learning community—"What do we want students to know and be able to do?"—they are laying the foundation for their work to increase achievement for all students.

In a traditional school, teachers work in isolation to decide what to teach. Each of the teachers at the same grade level puts a different emphasis on different parts of the curriculum. For example, one first-grade teacher in a school might believe that literacy is vitally important. She might use trade books to teach science and social studies and spend every extra minute of time immersing students in literacy. Another equally exceptional first-grade teacher in the same school might believe that while reading and writing are important, not all first graders are developmentally ready to be successful readers. She might provide lots of hands-on learning experiences that don't rely on reading skills for students to be successful. Yet another first-grade teacher might spend her extra time working on math facts, believing that, as students learn more complex algorithms, knowing facts will be important.

Any parent would want his or her child in the classroom of any of these remarkable teachers. When these students move on to second grade, they will have all been well-prepared—but each will have been prepared differently. The second-grade teacher must then fill in the gaps in some areas of each student's learning. As this scenario plays out over time, the preparation each student has for the next level of learning diverges more and more from that of other students in the same school, and teachers spend increasing amounts of instructional time filling in the gaps rather than moving forward with new learning.

On the other hand, imagine how a student might fare in a school like Woodlawn, where teachers have embraced the professional learning communities model. In a PLC, teacher teams work together to decide what skills and content are important for every student in that grade level or content area. They are very clear about what that learning looks like and how they will measure student proficiency. When students experience difficulty meeting a standard, the teacher team identifies ways to give that student more time and support to be successful. Teachers are still free to teach *how* they like—in ways they are comfortable, using strategies they are most adept at using—but they work together closely to make sure that *what* they teach is the same. When teachers in the same grade level agree about what to teach and what proficiency will look like in their grade level or content area, as they did at Woodlawn Middle School, all students enter the next grade level equally well-prepared.

What Research Says

In *What Works in Schools: Translating Research Into Action* (2003), Robert Marzano lists the factors that influence student achievement in schools based on his meta-analysis of the research. He concludes that the number-one school-level factor is a guaranteed and viable curriculum and identifies two critical aspects of viability: opportunity to learn and time to teach.

In his description of the first aspect, opportunity to learn, Marzano describes the differences between the *intended* curriculum, the *implemented* curriculum, and the *attained* curriculum. The intended curriculum is what the district or state develops, the implemented curriculum is what the teacher actually teaches, and the attained curriculum is what the student learns in the end. Providing all students the same opportunity to learn means that teacher teams must agree what matters most for their students to learn and on how they will align their assessment practices so that they will know whether the students know it. In fact, it's the difference between focusing on teaching and focusing on learning.

The second aspect of viability is whether or not teachers have enough time to teach the curriculum. Marzano suggests that the typical school year is far too short to allow teachers the time to teach the intended curriculum. As a result, they regularly make choices about what to include in their lessons. When teachers support the viability of their agreed-upon curriculum, they are saying that they believe it is likely that students can learn this material in the time set aside for it and that individual teachers won't have to "pick and choose" what to teach.

Given that a guaranteed and viable curriculum is the most important factor influencing student achievement, Marzano's research suggests that if collaborative teams of teachers work together to identify their essential outcomes, they can have a positive impact on the achievement of their students.

How to Identify Essential Outcomes

In the PLC model, essential outcomes or essential learnings are described as the "critical skills, knowledge, and dispositions each student must acquire as a result of each course, grade level and unit of instruction" (DuFour, DuFour, Eaker, & Many, 2006, p. 215). In his book *Power Standards* (2004), Larry Ainsworth discusses a process for deciding which state standards are the most essential in a school's curriculum—the "power" standards. In practice, power standards and essential outcomes refer to the same thing: specific descriptions about the content of the curriculum for a particular grade level or subject area. For our purposes, we will use these terms interchangeably.

Whether we call them power standards, grade-level expectations, performance descriptors, or essential learning, the desired product of this process is a very clear list of student learning outcomes for a given grade-level or content area. Reeves (2002) suggests that there shouldn't be more than a dozen for each grade-level content area.

Starting the Discussion

The first question teacher teams in a professional learning community discuss is "What do we want students to know and be able to do?" It is not unusual for teachers, even those who plan closely together, to mistakenly believe that they are all teaching the same curriculum in their classrooms. One activity that can help reveal teacher differences in a very nonthreatening way is for each teacher to independently answer the following two questions:

1. "What are five to seven essential understandings I want every student entering my classroom to have?"

2. "What are five to seven essential understandings I am willing to guarantee that every student leaving my classroom will have?"

The resulting discussion among team members will indicate some important answers about what's really important for students to know in a grade-level or content area. (Elementary teachers have found it more effective and efficient to consider one subject area at a time as they go through the process. Once they have finished the first subject area, subsequent subject areas go much more quickly.)

Once the discussion about what's really important has begun, teacher teams then gather the information they will use to determine the essential learning outcomes for their course or grade level. For example, they will need copies of their state standards, state assessment information, district curriculum guides, report cards, and perhaps even lesson plan books.

Checking Endurance, Leverage, and Readiness

Teacher teams then review the state standards developed for their grade level or content area. Often, state standards are very broadly written statements that encompass learning across several grade levels. These standards are then generally broken down by grade level. It is this list of specific grade-level expectations that teams will want to work from. Most teachers are familiar with their state standards and expectations, and they often believe that the state intends for them to put the same emphasis on each of these standards. The reality is that while each of these expectations is intended to be part of the curriculum, it is unlikely that they will all take the same amount of time or should receive the same emphasis by teachers as they teach and assess students. Through team discussion, then, teachers can agree on what each standard really means and what degree of emphasis should be placed on it in every classroom.

Teams use three criteria to identify power standards: endurance, leverage, and readiness for the next level of learning (Reeves, 2002). Some of the standards will fit only one of these criteria; others will fit more than one.

Endurance describes those standards that will be important to students beyond the time they are being taught and will be remembered after the assessment. One way to think about this is to consider what information adults easily remember from their own student learning experiences. Enduring standards *do not* include the kinds of facts and trivia that adults on the television show *Are You Smarter Than a Fifth Grader?* are embarrassed they've forgotten!

The second criterion for a power standard is leverage. *Leverage* describes those standards that identify knowledge or understanding across multiple subject areas. For example, being able to read and interpret charts and graphs is a skill often taught in math class and applied in science class. Many reading teachers now apply this skill as well—to the comprehension of technical reading material, for example.

The third criterion is readiness for the next level of learning. *Readiness* describes those standards that are prerequisite to future learning. For example, students must know sound-symbol relationships before they can apply phonics skills to decoding words.

After reviewing what endurance, leverage, and readiness for the next level of learning mean, teachers first individually determine for themselves which of the state performance descriptors or expectations fit those criteria. Just as teachers want their students to do some initial reflection in Think-Pair-Share, this step requires teachers to make some individual decisions about what they believe each outcome means. Teachers often find that some outcomes fit more than one of the three criteria.

Building Consensus

Next, the team works as a group to build consensus around what should be included on the final list of essential outcomes, keeping in mind Marzano's research on a guaranteed and viable curriculum to make sure they are creating a product that will work.

For some teams, the process of identifying essential outcomes is the first time a group decision is actually implemented by individual teachers behind their classroom doors. Decisions to include or exclude specific outcomes may require a teacher to add or eliminate units of study. When this kind of collaboration is new to school, getting to final consensus on essential outcomes can be hard, because the results require real change in our practice. For this specific reason, it is critical for the team to create team norms and consensus protocols that facilitate discussion and decision-making.

When consensus becomes difficult, asking a few practical questions can keep the team focused. For example, it is always important to review best-practice literature when discussing what to include. If a topic is controversial, ask, "What does research say?" Similarly, teachers can review the guidelines provided by the state department of education about high-stakes state tests and ask, "Will students be prepared to answer questions about content likely to be on the test?"

It is important that teachers are aware that using compromise rather than consensus can lead to difficulties down the line. Sometimes teachers will agree to include any of the standards or outcomes that team members think should be included; but if the list is too long, once the team puts the outcomes into practice, teachers will once again be making independent decisions about what's important and what not to include. Teams must constantly be asking themselves if their content is viable. Can the content be taught at the expected level of rigor in the time allowed? If not, the team needs to make the hard decisions about what to eliminate.

So, how can we work toward consensus? Here are some questions teams should ask themselves:

- "Is this the appropriate grade level or content area for this to be considered a power standard? Does it more appropriately belong somewhere else?"

- "If we eliminate this as a power standard, will the student still be able to learn the other material we believe is important?"

- "Am I including it because it's something I enjoy teaching rather than something I believe students must know?"

The last question is an important part in achieving consensus on essential outcomes. Doug Reeves challenges us to "pull the weeds" (2003, p. 52)—to eliminate activities that, although we enjoy teaching them and students enjoy doing them, do not match standards. (He also suggests that schools need to ensure maximum instructional time by eliminating schoolwide activities and assemblies that don't relate to the outcomes that have been identified as important.) In practice, this often remains an ongoing agenda item as teams plan together. Teachers know that when "pull the weeds" is on the agenda, they will be making sure that they are protecting instructional time—one of the two aspects of Marzano's guaranteed and viable curriculum.

Don't expect that everyone will agree without argument—debate will foster a better product during this time of discussion. As teachers share their thinking, the overall understanding of the team increases.

Ensuring Alignment

Once the group has come to consensus on their draft list, they examine the state testing guides to learn what is emphasized and included on the annual state test. Many states publish a table or blueprint showing what percentage of questions assess each standard. Teachers should determine if their list of essential outcomes fits a similar pattern (Ainsworth, 2004). For example, if a state emphasizes number sense at a particular grade level in math, the list of essential outcomes should also emphasize number sense. If teachers have never thoroughly examined practice tests or released items from the state test bank, they will learn a lot by actually taking one of the exams.

Alignment does not stop there, however. One goal of the process of determining essential learning is to remove overlap and gaps from a school's taught curriculum. By working as a team, teachers agree that they will all focus on the same important content. If the process stops there, the grade level will have eliminated redundancy and gaps, but the school may still see problems.

That means that an important next step is for teachers to review the work of other teachers who teach the same content at the grade levels above and below theirs. If the process of identifying essential standards has been scheduled for an embedded staff development session, and all the teams are working together at the same time, this can be accomplished by listing the draft essential learning outcomes on chart paper and posting them on the wall. Teachers then read the standards across grade levels to make sure all of the important content is included (Ainsworth, 2004). Often, teachers will see that two grade levels or subject areas have included the same or similar outcomes. These teams must then meet briefly to decide where the outcome best fits. For example, math teachers might teach the concept of slope, which might later be applied in science to reading a graph. Math will keep the standard on its chart as a prerequisite skill: Understanding slope meets the readiness criterion for a power standard in math. It may remain an outcome in science, but it might not be considered a power standard.

If the process of identifying essential outcomes is part of an ongoing process and teams are working individually during their team time, find a spot to post the draft outcomes together. Teams can then accomplish this vertical alignment piece at a time that's convenient for them, clearly marking the areas of overlap or gap for future conversation when the two teams can meet to resolve those questions.

Understanding Proficiency

Once teams have answered the first critical question of a professional learning community, "What do we want our students to know and be able to do?" they will be able to address the second critical question, "How will we know if they've learned?" by developing common assessments based on these essential outcomes.

But in order to move on, all teachers first must be clear about what the learning outcomes *mean*. What does proficiency look like? Throughout the process of defining essential outcomes, teams should be discussing how students will demonstrate that they have learned. For example, if students are expected to be able to write a focused essay, teachers must identify what a focused essay for their grade level would look like. What would be proficient? What would be better than proficient? Often teams will create collaborative scoring tools such as rubrics to come to consensus about proficiency. First, each teacher brings an essay that he or she feels fits each of the levels of the rubric for that standard. Second, the team reviews each of the essays and comes to agreement. Finally, they score essays together until they feel that each teacher is giving the same score for the same work.

Teams may find that using a process of unpacking or unwrapping their standards is helpful during this process. These discussions ask teacher teams to carefully study their essential outcomes to come to agreement about what that standard means and what proficiency will look like for that standard. Larry Ainsworth (2003) lays out one process for completing this task in his book *Unwrapping the Standards*; teachers who use Understanding by Design as their framework for curriculum design participate in similar discussions. Teams must reach agreement not only the essential outcomes, but also on how that will be measured: what students will be able to do (focusing on the verb in the standard) and what they will know (focusing on the nouns in the standard).

How to Use Your Essential Outcomes

Essential outcomes are an important first step for professional learning communities. Teams should consider how to *share their essential learning outcomes* with parents and colleagues. Many schools are publishing their lists on school homepages so that parents are aware of the most important outcomes for each grade and subject. Surprisingly, parents rarely disagree with the published list and are usually grateful to have the curriculum so clearly laid out for them.

Once you have completed the process of identifying essential outcomes and clarifying what proficiency looks like, you will also need to *develop a pacing guide* to ensure that teachers have agreement about the level of emphasis and rigor for each outcome. Create a monthly chart that displays the essential content that must be taught in that time period; be sure to consider the timing of high-stakes tests. For example, if the state test is given in February and you know that your third graders will be expected to write a persuasive essay, the unit on persuasive writing should be taught early enough in the school year to prepare students for that assessment.

Remember to *evaluate your outcomes* and your pacing guide. During the implementation phase, teams should continue to meet and discuss how the pacing guide is working, how successful their students are in meeting the outcomes, and what the data from common assessments reveals about their instruction. Over the year they will see how much more aligned their curriculum is and how their assessments can provide needed feedback for adjusting their instruction to the needs of their students. For example, teachers might find that they need to spend more time than they initially thought on a particular outcome, or preassessments might show that students have already mastered some of the content. Keep track of what worked and what didn't, examine any data that reveals the efficacy of your work, and revise your list of essential outcomes and your pacing guide accordingly.

Team Structures and Schedules

Schools have used various team configurations to accomplish the work of determining essential outcomes. Successful schools have always kept one thing in mind: Teams need to be made up of teachers who actually teach the subject or grade-level content being discussed. At the elementary level, most often the team includes all the teachers who teach that grade level. For very small schools that have only one teacher at a grade level, the team might be composed of the primary-level teachers in that building; they would then discuss and determine the essential outcomes for each of the primary grade levels together. Regardless of the size of the school, the process of developing essential outcomes must be collaborative. The discussion, debate, and consensus-building that occur ensure a better product.

Multiage schools will find that teams of teachers who teach the two or three grade levels that are combined under the structure of their programs must work closely together to identify the essential outcomes for their grade levels. For example, if there is a two-to-three loop, the teachers who teach those grade levels lay out the power standards for both grades. If a school combines both traditional grade levels and multiage classes, it is important that teachers of both structures agree on the essential outcomes for each of their grades. Students in multiage classes must have the same essential outcomes as those in traditional classes.

At the middle-school level, teachers who teach the same subject matter work together on their team. If a teacher teaches more than one subject area—a practice not uncommon in middle schools—he or she will work with one subject area during the process and help review for the other subject area during the review process. In small middle schools, teachers often work on subject-area teams that cross several grade levels. For example, a science team may work on the essential outcomes in science for all the grades in that school.

High school teams are designed around subject matter content. Teachers work on teams that teach the same course—for example, the Algebra I Team. Again, a teacher may be on more than one team for the discussion of essential outcomes but should be careful to participate in or review the outcomes for each of the courses she teaches.

Timing

There are several ways to structure when teams meet. Some schools ask teams to work during their team time to complete the process on an ongoing basis, and other schools bring the whole staff together at one time and finish the work during one full-day session. There are advantages and disadvantages to each strategy.

When the staff comes together to work on the project as embedded staff development, there is a clear focus on all teachers receiving the same instruction and following the same process. The project is completed expeditiously, and everyone on the staff is involved. Vertical articulation occurs as a part of the process when teachers display their grade or course standards, and the team looks at the entire list together. The disadvantage of this approach is that when the group breaks into small groups to examine subject areas, teachers who teach two subjects or levels must choose only one small group to attend.

By contrast, when teams meet on an ongoing basis during team time, teachers can participate on multiple teams: All teachers are involved in all meetings discussing their grade level or content area. As a result, the process takes longer. Additional time is also required to allow teams to review the draft lists of essential outcomes above or below their grade level to ensure vertical alignment.

No matter how a professional learning community organizes the process to answer the question, "What do we want students to know and be able to do?", it is essential to complete all steps in the process and to work as a collaborative team on the school level. This is not a task that can or should be accomplished by the district; it is a job best accomplished by teachers at the local level.

A Final Note

It is not uncommon for teachers beginning this collaborative process to express concern that they are losing their academic freedom. In truth, we are always part of the process of deciding what to include on our list of essential outcomes. Teachers in any school are expected to use state and national standards as a guideline. In a professional learning community our own experiences, the district's curriculum, and best-practice literature also play a key role in the decision-making process. Sometimes we do have to eliminate a favorite unit of study, but this usually reflects its misalignment with the curriculum. Once the essential outcomes are in place, teachers in a professional learning community are free to teach how they like, using strategies they feel are most appropriate, those they are most comfortable using, and those that will motivate their students.

Other teachers express concern that if they don't cover the entire curriculum, students won't be prepared for the state tests. Larry Ainsworth (2004) quotes Doug Reeves' response to this issue with the following insight: "What you will find is that a good set of Power Standards will cover about 88 percent of the items on the state test, but not 100 percent. If you go after the extra 12 percent, you will have to cover many more standards and hence have less teaching time to thoroughly teach each of the Power Standards" (p. 97). Most of us know there is simply too much to teach; the process of identifying essential outcomes allows us to focus our efforts where they matter most. In my experience, teachers who have identified essential outcomes report that they feel much more confident that their students are prepared for high-stakes testing, because they are working closely together as a school to align their curriculum from grade level to grade level and subject to subject.

Ultimately, understanding what we want kids to know and be able to do at each grade level and in each subject requires a collaborative effort. Individuals working in isolation cannot create lists of the same quality as a team of teachers engaged in rich discussions around what the standard means, what proficiency will look like, and what's most important to emphasize. This process takes time, and time is one of our most valuable resources in schools. But think about it: If we take time to lay the foundation of what matters most in our curriculum, subsequent decisions about assessment and interventions will be built on that solid foundation. We can then be assured our students really are learning at high levels!

References

Ainsworth, L. (2003). *"Unwrapping" the standards: A simple process to make standards manageable.* Englewood, CO: Advanced Learning Press.

Ainsworth, L. (2004). *Power standards: Identifying the standards that matter the most.* Engelwood, CO: Advanced Learning Press.

DuFour, R., DuFour, R., Eaker, R., & Many, T. (2006). *Learning by doing: A handbook for professional learning communities at work.* Bloomington, IN: Solution Tree.

Marzano, R. J. (2003). *What works in schools: Translating research into action.* Alexandria, VA: Association for Supervision and Curriculum Development.

Marzano, R. J., & Kendall, J. S. (1998). *Awash in a sea of standards.* Aurora, CO: Mid-continent Research for Education and Learning. Accessed at www.mcrel.org on September 25, 2007.

Reeves, D. B. (2002). *The leader's guide to standards: A blueprint for educational equity and excellence.* San Francisco: Jossey-Bass.

Reeves, D. B. (2003). *Making standards work: How to implement standards-based assessments in the classroom, school, and district.* Englewood, CO: Advanced Learning Press.

Schmoker, M., & Marzano, R. (1999). Realizing the promise of standards-based education. *Educational Leadership, 56,* 17–21. Accessed at www.ascd.org on October 1, 2007.

ERIC TWADELL

An award-winning practitioner, Eric Twadell, Ph.D., has used the Professional Learning Communities at Work model to direct curriculum, staff development, and mentoring programs at Adlai E. Stevenson High School District 125 in Lincolnshire, Illinois. He served as director of the school's social studies division and as assistant superintendent for organizational and leadership development before his promotion to district superintendent. Dr. Twadell's commitment to student achievement reaches beyond the academic setting through his directorship of numerous athletic and adventure education programs. Dr. Twadell works closely with schools and districts nationwide to advance the successful implementation of the PLC model. He has also consulted with both the Illinois State Board of Education and Missouri Department of Education.

FIVE

Instructional Improvement From the Inside Out: Lesson Study at Work

Eric Twadell

In schools that are moving along the continuum as a professional learning community, teachers are finding the old adage to be true: "Two heads are better than one." Working collaboratively in curriculum teams, teachers are finding new and innovative ways to develop lessons, improve their instructional practice, and engage students in meaningful learning opportunities.

In the professional learning community school, professional development is designed to support and build upon the collective capacity of teachers to work effectively as members of collaborative teams (DuFour & Eaker, 1998). The learning community actively seeks out professional development opportunities for collaborative teacher teams. These teams build shared knowledge and understanding on issues of curriculum, instruction, and assessment.

One of the most promising professional development initiatives for building collaborative relationships and for developing shared understanding among teachers on how to improve their instructional practice and student learning is Japanese lesson study (Lewis, 2002; Richardson, 2004; Stigler & Hiebert, 1999).

What Is Lesson Study?

Lesson study has long been an integral component of teacher professional development in Japanese schools. In *The Teaching Gap* (1999), Stigler and Hiebert describe how video data collected from the Third International Mathematics and Science Study (TIMSS) revealed that in Japanese schools, teachers have utilized lesson study as a systemic process for improving instruction. The traditional culture of continuous improvement in Japanese schools has led to the development of lesson study as a collaborative protocol for teachers to work together to examine their instructional practice and make improvements in their teaching (Stigler & Hiebert, 1999).

While traditional lesson planning focuses on "what teachers plan to teach," lesson study focuses more specifically on "what teachers want students to learn" (Richardson, 2004, p. 5). The difference is significant. Lesson study is a systematic process in which teachers work interdependently to strengthen their individual and collective ability to improve instruction and increase student learning. Makoto Yoshida has described lesson study as a process in which "teachers work collaboratively to carefully craft a lesson. They will meet several times as a group to draft a plan for this lesson and ultimately one of the teachers in the group will teach the lesson with all other group members present in the classroom. The teachers will then reflect on lesson implementation and try out improvements by having a second group member teach a revised version of the lesson" (Yoshida, 1999, p. 6). The strong emphasis on collaboration and collective inquiry in the Japanese lesson study process enables and supports the ongoing work of teachers in the professional learning community who are learning together how to improve their practice.

The Lesson Study Process

While the length of the lesson study may vary, the lesson study cycle typically includes the following steps (adapted from Carter,

2003; Lewis, 2002; Stigler & Hiebert, 1999; Stepanek, Appel, Leong, Mangan, & Mitchell, 2007).

Establish the Learning Goal

An effective lesson study begins when a collaborative team of teachers identifies a student learning goal for the upcoming lesson. Teams can develop goals on identified gaps in student achievement data, or they may create goals that reflect the instructional priorities identified in their school, department, or grade-level vision statement, such as reading or critical thinking (Carter, 2003; NCREL, 2002).

Research the Lesson

Once the team establishes a learning goal, teachers must conduct research to collect information and data that will support the collaborative lesson planning process. Teams must choose the unit in which the lesson will be taught and research potential content and skills that will be incorporated into the lesson to support the learning goal. Teams may also wish to examine instructional strategies that have been successful in helping students achieve the learning goal.

Plan the Lesson

Next, teams collaboratively plan the student lesson, incorporating their research on successful instructional strategies that will support their established learning goal. The lesson plan outlines and details all the activities that will be facilitated during the class period (NCREL, 2002). Teams also make hypotheses and predictions on how students will demonstrate their understanding and learning of the articulated instructional goal (Carter, 2003). Based on the anticipated student responses, teams identify what data the observing teachers will collect while the lesson is being facilitated.

Teach the Lesson

The team collaboratively decides who will present the lesson first. While one teacher facilitates the lesson, other team members take notes and collect data based on the hypotheses and predictions the team made on how students shall demonstrate understanding of the established learning goal. The observing teachers may also document the lesson through the use of video, photographs, audiotapes, and student work (NCREL, 2002).

Reflect and Evaluate

After the lesson, the team meets to debrief. The teacher who facilitated the lesson shares his or her impressions first, then the other teachers present their observations and share data they collected during the lesson. The team focuses on those data and observations that might provide evidence that the established student learning goal was met as a result of the lesson (Lewis, 2002).

Revise the Lesson

Based on the team's observations and interpretation of the collected data, the team revises to the lesson plan. The team may change everything from the warm-up activities to the materials used or to the questions asked during the lesson (Stigler & Hiebert, 1999). The revised lesson will address the gaps in student understanding and learning identified during the implementation of the first lesson.

Reteach the Lesson

Once the team has revised the lesson to more effectively achieve the established student learning goal, a different member of the team presents the revised lesson to a different class of students. Team members will again take notes and collect data to determine the extent to which the revised lesson was able to help students achieve the learning goal. At this stage, the lesson may be facilitated in front of a larger group of observers. In some Japanese schools, the presentation of the revised lesson is open to all teachers within the school, and an outside expert may be invited to observe (Stigler & Hiebert, 1999).

Reflect and Evaluate After Reteaching

Afterwards, the whole group discusses and evaluates the presentation of the revised lesson by reviewing observation notes and analyzing the collected data to assess student learning. Team members work to build shared knowledge of how the lesson facilitated student understanding of the student learning goal. If the team feels that the lesson needs further refinement, a third member of the team may present a further revision of the lesson, with subsequent reflection and evaluation.

Share the Results

The lesson study is not complete without a public presentation of the team's lesson. The lesson and findings may be shared in several ways, such as a written report, a presentation at a department or faculty meeting, or the addition of the lesson to the school's bank of teacher resources (Stigler & Hiebert, 1999). Public sharing of results is a significant component of the lesson study process (Stepanek et al., 2007). This presentation includes the team's reflections and learning on the components of the lesson that helped students to achieve the established learning goals as well as the broader implications for how to improve instructional practice to ensure student learning.

A Story of Lesson Study at Work

In a professional learning community, teachers collaborate on a regular basis to explore new ideas and strategies to improve their instructional practice. While such collective inquiry may take a variety of forms, participation in a structured lesson study process provides teachers with the opportunity to work together to explore a lesson from the inside out. Working together, teachers learn how to design, implement, measure, and improve upon their collaborative developed lesson plans and instructional strategies. The following story attempts to illustrate one curriculum team's journey in a lesson study process.

Coming back after what seemed like a very short summer, Anne was looking forward to the 3 staff development days her school provided for departments and curriculum teams to meet before students arrived. Anne had found that time to be a great opportunity for teachers to work and plan together for the year ahead.

Given the strong commitment to working as a professional learning community in Anne's school, it came as no surprise when near the end of the first social studies department meeting, Jim, the department chair, announced that he would be looking for a few volunteers from the world history team to participate in a lesson study.

"What's lesson study?" one of the new hires asked.

"Well, in general terms," Jim said, "lesson study is an opportunity for a team to work together to create and refine a lesson to achieve a certain learning objective. You'll plan a lesson together, then one person from your team will teach the lesson while the others observe. You'll revise the lesson based on your observations and then reteach the revised version of the lesson to a different group of students." Knowing that teachers were anxious to move on to their curriculum team meetings, Jim ended the meeting by asking that any world history teacher who might be interested in learning more about the lesson study process meet in his office the next morning.

Anne realized that although she was a little nervous when other teachers observed her own classes, she always enjoyed watching other teachers in their classrooms. Lesson study would provide an interesting opportunity to observe some of the more veteran members of her world history team. Of the 12 members of the team, 5 teachers met with Jim the next morning. Anne was grateful that Jim had personally asked Amy and Eduardo, two of the more experienced and veteran members of the team, to participate in the lesson study. Both Amy and Eduardo were respected throughout the department for their deep understanding of history and their ability to connect with students. Anne was also happy to see that Steve decided to come to the meeting. Anne and Steve had become quick friends during their first year together in the department. Everyone was surprised to see Lee, a first-year teacher. "I'm a little overwhelmed," Lee admitted, "but I want to give this lesson study thing a try!"

As the meeting began, Jim thanked everyone for coming to the meeting and for their willingness to try something new. He also shared that since he was no expert, they would all be learning more about lesson study together. Jim distributed three articles about Japanese lesson study that he had read over the summer and asked if everyone was comfortable taking 20 minutes or so to read them over before discussing them as a group. Each of the articles described how lesson study grew out of Japan's strong culture of continuous improvement and showed it has become the preferred method of collaboration and teacher learning.

As they discussed the lesson study process, everyone was a little surprised that the typical lesson study cycle was approximately a month, with some cycles lasting up to a year. Anne was relieved that Lee asked the question she couldn't get off her mind as she read the articles and listened to the conversation: "You mean we're going to spend all this time on just one lesson?"

Smiling, Jim said, "Yep! Why not?"

Although the group still had more questions than answers, everyone decided that like Lee, they would "give it a try." Knowing that the lesson study process usually begins by establishing a learning goal, Jim asked that before their next meeting, everyone on the team think about a possible goal for their lesson study.

Anne didn't quite know what to expect when the group met for their first lesson study meeting. She remembered that Jim had asked that everyone think about a learning goal, but in the craziness of the first week, she didn't have time to think carefully about it. She was relieved to find that when Jim polled the group, no one else had been able to give serious thought to a goal for the lesson study, either.

"Well, why don't we brainstorm some ideas?" Jim suggested.

There was silence. No one seemed to know where to begin. Sensing the growing frustration, Jim finally said, "Maybe the most appropriate place to start would be the vision statement we wrote as a department 2 years ago." Some of the most exciting meetings Anne attended during her first years as a teacher were the department meetings to articulate what a world-class social studies department would be like. The team had studied the National Council for Social Studies Teaching Standards and created a vision statement that identified teaching and learning as powerful when they are meaningful, challenging, value-based, integrated, and active.

Jim read the vision statement aloud to the group.

"You know," Eduardo remarked, "a lot of the questions and discussions we had back then centered on the integration standard. We talked a lot about what an effective lesson would look like if it was truly integrated."

"I remember that," Amy said. "But it's been almost 3 years since we wrote the vision statement, and it doesn't seem like we're any closer as a department to developing a shared understanding of how to create a daily lesson or unit plan that focuses on integration."

Steve suggested that since the department was continuing to struggle with integration, maybe their team should focus on developing a lesson study that would explore how to effectively integrate content and skills into a world history lesson. Anne was impressed with how quickly the group came to consensus on the learning goal. Privately, she wondered whether all of the group's decisions would be that easy. As the meeting ended, Jim reminded the group that the next step in the lesson study process involved conducting research and asked everyone to think about a unit and topic for the lesson study.

At the next meeting, it was clear that consensus would not come as easily as it did the week before. Everyone had a different idea for the unit and the lesson. While Anne wanted to focus on comparing and contrasting the Western religions, Amy was hoping to teach more geographical literacy. Eduardo was interested in stretching students' understanding about Rome, Steve wanted to focus on feudalism, and as a first-year teacher, Lee was just looking to stay a unit ahead of the students. Although Jim didn't quite expect such widely divergent thinking, he blamed himself for not asking the teachers to work together in conducting their research. Jim knew from experience that when working in isolation, teachers tend to focus on areas of *interest*, which may or may not be areas of student *need*.

"It looks like this issue will be hard to decide," Jim said. "Why don't we look at our formative and summative assessments for some clues?"

Although the overall average on the first semester final exam was impressive at 82%, the subtest on the Renaissance caused the team concern. Students always seemed to have problems with the unit on the Renaissance, but the last group of students to take the exam really struggled—their average on the Renaissance subtest of the exam was 63%. As the team talked about the results, they agreed that focusing their lesson study on the Renaissance was clearly in the best interests of their students.

Based on his reading of lesson study, Jim knew that the next step in the cycle would need the most time. After finding a common date for the team to meet, Jim arranged for substitutes so that the team could spend an entire day working together to collaboratively plan a lesson for the Renaissance unit. "Don't worry about bringing any materials to the planning day," he told the team. "I'll bring everything we'll need."

On the day of the planning, Jim greeted each teacher outside the room and gave them the only materials they could use for the first part of the morning: a pad of paper and two pencils. A little stunned, the group looked at Jim for some direction.

"That's it?" Lee said. "You want us to plan a lesson with just paper and pencils?"

"After all my years of teaching and serving as a department chair, I've come to the realization that when teachers sit down to plan a unit or a lesson, we tend to look first to all of the wrong places," Jim said.

After a moment, Anne smiled. "You mean the textbook?"

"And the calendar, and the file cabinet of old lessons," Amy added.

The team agreed that these things often served as distractions during the lesson planning process, and that in a professional learning community, learning should always serve as the primary influence in lesson planning. By removing some of the traditional teaching-centered tools, Jim helped the team focus clearly on their learning goal of creating a lesson that focused on integration. Jim told the team he would check back in a couple of hours to see how they were doing.

Amy, a 26-year veteran and a natural leader, quickly got everyone on task. As the team had already decided to focus the lesson on the Renaissance, Amy asked the group to consider how they might be able to create a lesson that stressed the integration of content and skills. Most of the early conversation reviewed lessons that each of the teachers had created in the past, so Amy asked each teacher to write down something about the Renaissance that students seemed to have difficulty understanding. As the team talked through their responses, they realized that while they may have been teaching different lessons, students in all of their classes were having difficulty understanding how the writing and art of the Renaissance period was an integration and reflection of styles from the Greek and Roman and the Byzantine and Middle Ages periods.

The team dialogued on what they wanted students to learn about the influence of earlier cultures and historical periods on Renaissance art. As the informal facilitator of the team, Amy kept a record of the conversation. Once the team had identified the specific concepts and ideas they wanted students to learn as a result of the lesson, they worked to identify instructional strategies that might support their learning targets. Midway through the morning, they took a short break.

Anne took Steve aside in the hall. "I'm embarrassed to admit it, but for me, the question of what to teach usually comes second—after I figure out how I'll teach and how much time I have to do it." She sighed. "Now I'm beginning to understand what Jim meant in my postobservation conferences when he suggested that I needed to start my unit and lesson planning 'with the end in mind.'"

After more intense discussion and planning, the team decided to develop a lesson to review the artwork examined early in the semester and help students understand how the art of the Renaissance was a reflection of earlier cultures and periods. To do so, the team spent most of the day pulling together art slides and developing a Power Point presentation in which they would show representations of art from the Greek, Roman, Byzantine, and Middle Ages periods and ask students to describe how the pieces influenced select art representations from the Renaissance era.

When they completed the lesson plan, the team felt very good about their collective work. Anne thought that the dialogue about which pieces of Renaissance art to utilize and their historical influences was absolutely fascinating, and Steve enjoyed hearing Eduardo and Amy share some of their instructional ideas. It was clear, however, that Lee still had some questions.

"Look, I know I'm just a rookie," he said, "and I think the lesson is going to be great, but I'm still struggling with the question that Jim asked us to consider earlier. How will we know if students actually learn all of this stuff?"

Lee's question stumped the group. As the team shared their usual assessment strategies, they realized that more often than not, each waited to the end of a unit to assess whether students had learned the concepts and skills presented in class. The team agreed that waiting for the next exam would not provide the immediate feedback they needed to be able to improve upon the lesson and provide interventions for students who were not learning.

In order to assess student learning during the lesson, the team decided to develop observation rubrics. Rubrics would help them measure student progress toward the established learning goal. "Okay, let's summarize," Amy said. "Our hypothesis is that we'll be able to determine the extent to which students understood the lesson if we closely examine the following criteria." She wrote them on the white board.

1. Each question the teacher asks during the lesson

2. The amount of time each slide is shown to the students

3. The participation patterns of the students

4. Whether student responses show basic recall or higher-order critical thinking skills

"Sounds right to me," Eduardo said. "I think the amount of time is especially important since we've identified 63 slides that we want to show students."

At the end of the day, the team met with Jim to review their lesson. "It looks great," he said. "Who's going to teach it first?"

After an awkward pause, Eduardo volunteered to teach the lesson to his first period world history class. A 23-year veteran who had taught nearly every course in the department and served as a mentor to many new teachers, Eduardo was comfortable having his colleagues observe his teaching. In fact, he felt that as a successful veteran teacher, he had a professional obligation to work with his colleagues and to help them improve their craft. Jim thanked Eduardo for volunteering and let the group know that he would schedule substitutes so that Amy, Anne, Lee, and Steve would be able to observe Eduardo teach the lesson the following week.

On the day of the lesson, Eduardo was surprised to find himself a little unnerved. Amy, Anne, Steve, and Lee had spread themselves around the room so that they each could take notes and collect data. Eduardo's comfort level returned as he facilitated the warm-up activity that the team had developed. Sensing that students were ready to move on to the lesson, Eduardo started the team's PowerPoint presentation. As the first slides were representations of Greek and Roman art, students were quick to identify the pieces and the era they were from. Eduardo was pleased to see students continued to participate at high levels as the presentation moved through the different eras. By the end of the period, as students completed a short writing activity on how art from earlier eras influenced Renaissance artists, Eduardo was feeling very good about the lesson and the high levels of student participation.

The group met in Jim's office the next morning to reflect on the lesson and review their notes and observation rubrics. Although Jim had decided not to observe Eduardo teach, fearing his role as supervisor might influence the lesson, he was very excited to be a part of the reflection and evaluation of the lesson. He started the debriefing by asking a question that he later decided he would never ask again: "So, Eduardo, how did it go?"

It was clear to everyone that Eduardo was as excited a day later as he was immediately after the lesson. Eduardo summarized the lesson for Jim, sharing how well the warm-up activity went, the fact that students identified nearly every piece of art, and that students remarked after class how much they enjoyed the lesson.

As Eduardo recalled the lesson, Anne couldn't help noticing that the more excited Eduardo got, the deeper into their chairs the others members of the team sank. When Eduardo finished reviewing the lesson, Jim asked another question that he later vowed never to ask again: "So, what did you guys think?"

Jim was caught off guard by the long pause before anyone responded. Jim had fully expected the other members of the group to share Eduardo's enthusiasm for the lesson, but he quickly realized that the observation data was going to tell a different story. "Alright," Jim said, "how about if each of you shares the data you collected and the notes you took during the observation?"

As the team shared their observations and reviewed the results of the student writing activity, it became clear that the lesson did not achieve the established learning goal: Students were not able to identify how representations of Renaissance art were influenced by earlier cultures and periods.

What Eduardo heard from his colleagues was utterly inconsistent with how he felt after the lesson. "How can this be?" he said. "Can I look at the rubrics?"

After taking a few minutes to review the four observation rubrics, Eduardo was stunned. The rubric that tallied the total number of student responses was overflowing with check marks, but the rubric that tracked the number of higher order and critical thinking responses was completely blank. Although students were fully participating, their responses were focused on the wrong ideas.

"One of the reasons I felt so good after the lesson was because of all of the students who were participating," Eduardo said. "In fact, for as long as I can remember, on any given day, I've used the criteria of 'Did I finish the lesson?' and 'Were my students engaged?' to determine the success of my teaching."

Eduardo was not alone. As the discussion continued, it became clear to the group that day in and day out, each teacher tended to gauge the success of daily lessons based primarily on the level of student engagement and whether the lesson was completed by the end of the class period.

Although Jim was happy the team recognized that student responses were not at the level that would suggest they learned the intended outcomes for the lesson, he was unsure if the group had identified why. Steve shared that his responsibility during the observation was to write down every question that Eduardo asked during the class period. When the group reviewed the log, they found a consistent pattern. All of the questions Eduardo asked were focused on identifying pieces of art, rather than eliciting responses that integrated knowledge across the units and periods of study.

"Someone once told me, 'If you ask a recall question, you get a recall response,'" Eduardo said. "I guess this proves it."

Feeling that they had a good idea of how to improve upon their collective work, the team decided to meet the following week to plan a revised version of the lesson.

Making improvements and revisions to the existing lesson was much easier than starting from scratch. The team made one simple change: To ensure that students were being asked to focus on the higher order skills of integrating units of study, the team decided to write out every question that the teacher would ask during the lesson. Steve volunteered to teach the revised lesson to his seventh period world history class, and the team decided to utilize the same observation rubrics.

As the warm-up activity the team created worked well for Eduardo, Steve began the lesson in the same way. Then he used the team's scripted questions to guide the discussion. Steve was a little taken back by the breadth and depth of students' comments. Student responses did reflect the higher-order thinking the team was hoping for, but Steve knew *exactly* what the team was going to say in the reflection and evaluation.

Eager to discuss and debrief, the team decided to meet immediately after school with Jim.

"Well, that was interesting," Lee said.

Amy agreed: "I really didn't expect that."

Not having seen the lesson, Jim was a little confused. "What happened?"

Steve shared that while the students did a great job in the discussion, as reflected in the observation rubrics, he was nowhere near finishing the lesson. In fact, the discussion was so good, and the student responses were so in-depth, they were only able to get through the representations of Greek and Roman art—they didn't even get a chance to talk about the Renaissance. As the team reviewed the observation rubrics, it became clear that by identifying exactly what questions they wanted to ask about the pieces of art, students were responding with the integrated understanding the team was seeking. So Steve would finish the lesson the next day in class.

When the team met to revise the lesson again, they decided on a number of changes. First, the team decided that before Anne facilitated the lesson in her class, she would give her students a homework assignment that included all of the art pieces and the corresponding questions that would be asked during the class period. The team hypothesized that if students had already analyzed the art before class, their responses in homework would reflect more integrated understanding. In addition, the team decided that given the breadth and depth of the discussion in Steve's class, it was probably better to teach the lesson over a 2-day period than to rush the discussion within a single class period. Lastly, the team decided to change the writing activity that students would complete at the end of the class to more thoroughly and specifically assess student's understanding of how Renaissance art was influenced by earlier cultures and historical periods.

When it was Anne's turn to deliver the lesson, she found it odd that she wasn't as nervous as she usually was to have colleagues observing in her classroom. She was actually looking forward to it. Anne had come to enjoy the time she was spending with the lesson study team and trusted that they were as interested as she was in improving their professional practice.

The revised lesson was a success. In fact, in her 3 short years of teaching, Anne could not remember a lesson in which she was more confident that students had actually learned the intended outcomes. In their final debriefing meeting, the team reviewed the observation rubrics, their notes from the lesson, and the student's written responses. The data confirmed the group's general feeling that their lesson was a wonderful learning opportunity for students. To celebrate and share their success, they presented their lesson and the results at the next department meeting.

Benefits of Japanese Lesson Study in a Professional Learning Community

Anne's story in this chapter illustrates what a growing body of research also demonstrates: the powerful effect that lesson study can have on teaching and learning (Lewis, 2002; Stepanek et al., 2007). Lesson study requires teachers to work together interdependently as members of a collaborative team in order to improve upon their individual and collective ability to increase student learning and achievement. Within the professional learning community, the lesson study process serves as a powerful vehicle to promote continuous improvement, collaboration, a focus on student learning, self-directed teacher learning, and professional development.

Continuous Improvement

Teachers engaged in lesson study are actively involved in a continuous improvement model. Continuous improvement in the professional learning community is not last year's initiative; it is an every year initiative. The traditional school was not designed to support ongoing professional learning and improvement; in a professional learning community, however, the lesson study cycle enables a systematic process of research and reflection of effective instructional practices that will enhance a teacher's professional practice on an ongoing basis (Stepanek et al., 2007).

Collaboration

Teachers engaged in lesson study work interdependently as members of a collaborative team. Rick DuFour has described collaboration as the sine qua non of the professional learning community. Effective collaboration in a learning community requires more than teachers just working *near* one another; they must begin working *with* one another. The lesson study process enables teachers to work together interdependently to explore "each other's experience and expertise, and build a shared knowledge of professional practice" (NCREL, 2002, p.iii).

A Focus on Student Learning

Teachers engaged in lesson study maintain a laser-like focus on student learning. In the professional learning community, every effort is made to establish learning rather than teaching as the guiding principle decision in decisions of curriculum, instruction, and assessment. The ongoing reflection and evaluation inherent in the lesson study process is tied to the established student learning goal. Success measures the extent to which teachers have helped students master the intended outcomes for the lesson. The lesson study process encourages teachers to gather evidence and evaluate the success of their lessons on demonstrated achievement of specific and measurable learning outcomes within the context of the lesson rather than waiting for an end of unit quiz or test.

Self-Directed Teacher Learning

Teachers engaged in lesson study direct their own learning of their subject matter and effective instruction. Lesson study is a systematic process to improve teacher's instructional practice, not an effort to fill a file cabinet with lesson and unit plans (NCREL, 2002). The fundamental assumption of lesson study is that *teacher learning* is the key to student learning. Through collective inquiry, intensive research, study, and lesson preparation, teachers develop a deeper understanding of their content knowledge (Lewis, Perry, & Hurd, 2004). The lesson planning process—as well as the collaborative observations, data and evidence gathering, and lesson revision—is a wonderful opportunity for teachers to also develop a deeper understanding of the characteristics of effective instruction (Lewis et al., 2004).

Professional Development

Teachers engaged in lesson study model the characteristics of effective professional development. As opposed to the "sit and get" model of a traditional school's professional development efforts, lesson study engages teachers in reflection and research on effective instruction in the context of their daily teaching and on-going work with students (Stigler & Hiebert, 1999). Lesson study reflects a professional development model consistent with the National Staff Development Council's *Standards for Staff Development* (2001) and engages teachers in "effective professional learning" on a daily basis within the context of their practice.

The lesson study process provides teachers working in collaboration with a unique opportunity to spend time carefully planning a detailed lesson and working together to critically analyze its effectiveness with a deep knowledge of how the lesson was designed to work—from the inside out. At a time when much of the discussion in many schools focuses on the negative impacts of AYP, lesson study provides a wonderful opportunity for teachers to become students as they *learn together* how to improve upon their daily work and instructional practice.

References

Carter, J. (2003, September). Personal interview. Lincolnshire, IL: Adlai E. Stevenson High School.

DuFour, R., & Eaker, R. (1998). *Professional learning communities at work: Best practices for enhancing student achievement*. Bloomington, IN: Solution Tree (formerly National Educational Service).

Lewis, C. (2002). *Lesson study: A handbook of teacher-led instructional change*. Philadelphia: Research for Better Schools.

Lewis, C., Perry, R., & Hurd, J. (2004). A deeper look at lesson study. *Educational Leadership, 61*(5), 18–22.

National Staff Development Council. (2001). *Standards for Staff Development*. Oxford, OH: Author.

North Central Regional Educational Laboratory (NCREL). (2002). *Teacher to teacher: Reshaping instruction through lesson study*. Naperville, IL: Author.

Richardson, J. (2004, February/March). Lesson study: Teachers learn how to improve instruction. *Tools for Schools*. Oxford, OH: National Staff Development Council.

Stigler, J., & Hiebert, J. (1999). *The teaching gap: Best ideas from the world's teachers for improving instruction in the classroom*. New York: Free Press

Stepanek, J., Appel, G., Leong, M., Mangan, M., & Mitchell, M. (2007). *Leading lesson study: A practical guide for teachers and facilitators*. Thousand Oaks, CA: Corwin.

Yoshida, M. (1999). *Lesson study: A case study of a Japanese approach to improving instruction through school-based teacher development*. Unpublished doctoral dissertation, University of Chicago, Illinois.

DENNIS KING

The Blue Valley School District in Overland Park, Kansas, is an impressive example of effective school improvement. This district has built professional learning communities in all of its 31 schools (4 high schools, 8 middle schools, and 19 elementary schools). One of the crucial driving forces behind this process has been district assistant superintendent of school improvement, Dennis King, Ed.D. Under his leadership, the 1,300 students and 120 staff members of Blue Valley High School (BVHS) have realigned their mission and vision to fit the PLC model. Resulting gains on national, state, and local assessments have been tremendous; the school has received the Standard of Excellence in math, reading, and writing for the past 7 years. Additionally, the Blue Valley School District was selected as a best-practice district by the American Productivity and Quality Center (APQC) and the Data Quality Campaign (DQC). The nomination recognized Blue Valley's effective, unique approach to fostering and implementing professional learning communities throughout the district.

SIX

Connecting Curriculum Mapping to Assessment for Learning

Dennis King

Historically, school improvement initiatives often start with small, isolated steps at one school within the district. A group of teachers who teach the same grade level or content might tinker with new ideas and occasionally they may even go so far as to actually implement new practices. Too often, however, these innovations dry up and wither due to lack of support within the school or district culture. Outliers such as these teachers find themselves subject to the law of survival of the fittest, and they are rarely able to sustain their improvements over time.

Similarly, district or school initiatives rarely permeate classroom walls to enhance student learning within an entire school or whole district. As teachers, we are continually asked to juggle various school improvement initiatives—sometimes developed by committees and handed down to us to implement—to enhance our classroom practice. We struggle to find time to collaborate with our colleagues to improve student learning by engaging in conversations on curriculum, assessment, and instructional strategies. We struggle to create an environment in which we support each other and learn from one another. Too often we make statements such as, "Our plate is full—we can't do one more new thing."

The process of becoming a professional learning community can build this missing bridge between the broader school improvement initiative and our daily practices in classrooms. Creating shared understanding through ongoing conversations about student learning is essential to connect our school improvement efforts in our classrooms and schools. This chapter will explore how focusing the collaborative work of grade-level or departmental teams on the process of curriculum mapping can enhance our teaching and student learning. We will examine how to close the gap between the written curriculum and the taught curriculum, how to identify the content and skills necessary to achieve the desired standard, and how to create assessments for learning that align with our curriculum and standards. Curriculum mapping and assessment for learning are research-based school improvement initiatives that focus our work on the essentials of learning and the critical questions of a professional learning community.

The Curriculum Journey

In *What Works in Schools* (2003), Robert Marzano identifies two types of curricula that are typically found in schools: the written curriculum, and the implemented or taught curriculum. Typically, all new teachers receive the written curriculum from the school or school district during their first days on the job. Those new to the profession may also participate in a step-by-step mentoring program with a master teacher.

In many schools, however, teacher understanding of the written curriculum stops at this point. Too often, teachers have little opportunity to discuss the transformation of the written curriculum into coherent lessons—the taught curriculum. Pfeffer and Sutton (2000) point out that we often work diligently on *knowing* or understanding a concept, but then fail to provide support for *doing*—for integrating what we've learned into daily practice. In other words, we fail to close the knowing-doing gap; we fail to integrate the written curriculum into a viable taught curriculum in our classrooms. Instead of discussing with our colleagues whether our students learned the written curriculum, we discuss what we taught, how lessons went, what we would like to teach in our classrooms—with little attention to whether the lessons align with the actual written curriculum.

As a high school biology teacher, I, too, was faced with this dilemma. I was given the district curriculum at the beginning of the school year. I read through the curriculum with my colleagues at a district inservice. Later I faced the challenge of implementation. Throughout my 9-year tenure as a classroom teacher in two different school systems, I approached the curricula in the same manner. Thank goodness the curriculum was aligned to our textbook—or was it? Was the textbook just full of information that happened to cover content with which I was the most familiar? I was constantly on a mission to develop more activities to engage my students in the class, but all too often, I did not reflect upon the actual content that I was teaching in relationship to any content standard. I seldom, if ever, identified skills that students should be able to perform within the curriculum. The integrity of the written curriculum was totally dependent upon my conscious effort and skills as a teacher. Like most of my peers, and like most teachers in traditional schools, I made teaching decisions based upon my own abilities, interests, and content knowledge, rather than the curriculum that was written for my students.

The gap between the taught and written curriculum is even more profound in the context of an entire school system; students in the same course or at the same grade level with another teacher experienced a very different curriculum than my students. This ever-increasing disconnect illustrates the need for curriculum mapping, the process that answers the first question of a professional learning community: "What do we want all students to know and be able to do?" (DuFour, DuFour, Eaker, & Many, 2006)

As we begin to clarify *what we want students to learn,* a systematic process focusing on the taught curriculum is essential. Though we may work together for years, we usually have sketchy knowledge about what goes on in each other's classrooms (Jacobs, 1997). By sharing structured, focused conversations within a collaborative, goal-oriented team—in which we record and discuss what we are actually teaching and what students are actually learning, across grade levels and courses—we greatly increase our professional skill.

As we begin to explore the curriculum issue, we have to question: Has our practice been so privatized that we are making decisions in isolation? Or are we in that rare situation where we can collaborate around the taught curriculum, refining alignment with written curriculum and standards as we focus precisely on what we want students to know and to be able to do?

Curriculum Mapping Challenges

Curriculum mapping is a widespread school improvement initiative that can be found in many schools and systems throughout North America and the world, thanks to experts like Heidi Hayes Jacobs and her colleagues Susan Udelhofen and Janet Hale. They built the collaborative foundation that allows us to develop structures for critical curriculum conversations. In the curriculum mapping process, every teacher collects data on the taught content and skills, assessments, and other critical aspects of learning to create a map of his or her classroom curriculum. Then we share maps with our colleagues to identify gaps and redundancies in teaching and learning. Our curriculum maps record the taught curriculum in every classroom in each school in the district. When maps are shared and collaboratively enhanced across schools in a district, we see a more consistent curriculum within and across schools: a curriculum that is ultimately aligned to standards and responsive to student data and other school initiatives (Udelhofen, 2005).

The mapping process is a two-step process designed to narrow the knowing-doing gap as it relates to curriculum implementation. In the first step, teachers record in diary format what is being taught in their classrooms: the actual content, skills, and assessment implemented. This initial step lays the foundation for the second step, when collaborative teams reflect and discuss potential improvements in content, skills, and assessments. These changes are recorded in the map, which then becomes a projection map for future teaching. These enhanced projection maps reduce the gap between the written and taught curriculum.

However, as I work with school districts across North America, I find the curriculum mapping initiative presents challenges for teachers as we reflect upon our own work in a diary map or as we collaborate to develop projection maps for our grade-level or content-area team. Most schools and districts struggle to begin a sustainable mapping process. In the first 3 years of mapping the curriculum, we often react to the ongoing data collection with questions such as, "Why do we have to do this?" and "Doesn't anyone know that I've been teaching everyday?" When faced with these questions, some schools are prone to abandon the work and retreat to the world of private teaching behind closed doors.

In those situations, curriculum mapping may lack coherence or meaning within a school or district. Schools and school districts may have developed annual curriculum calendars or guides for pacing teaching. Pacing guides provide an outline for curriculum pacing or implementation, but they still fail to ensure that any specific content or skill is actually part of the taught curriculum within our classrooms. These guides are often archived documents that simply do not reflect the reality of learning in the classroom. In a recent meeting of a group of science teachers who used a pacing guide, for example, individuals made comments like, "We have been doing this work for years." After further discussion, however, the teachers realized that although they had been swapping *activities* over the last 10 years, they lacked the opportunity to identify the content and skills needed to teach and support *a specific standard within the curriculum.*

The tradition of swapping activities or experiences does promote collegiality. We enjoy coming together to learn about and share new activities, and activities *are* important to support the content and skills found within a map. However, activities are not the driving force of a curriculum map. Sharing activities does not lead to documentation of and reflection on the necessary content and skills.

Using the Map as a Data Tool

In essence, a curriculum map provides a location to house our teaching data. The process of creating the map requires a shift in our thinking about how the curriculum is perceived, developed, and practiced. It makes each individual teacher's taught curriculum public, reviewable, and transparent. As a result, "the curriculum is no longer an action that occurs in isolation based upon the teacher's desires, but rather it becomes meaningful information that is shared with colleagues in an interactive forum to improve student learning" (Udelhofen, 2005, p. 9).

This cultural shift reinforces the collaborative work of the team as teachers begin to share and record the actual concepts to be taught in relationship to the written curriculum or standard. Teachers use the map 1) to define the essential question they want students to answer pertaining to that standard and 2) to identify the content and skills students must learn to support the standard. Simply put, the map provides a crystal-clear view of the student's curricular experience. The curriculum map contains what Robert Marzano (2003) identifies as the viable and taught curriculum, an essential step to improve student learning.

The cultural shift from traditional curriculum management systems or guides to curriculum maps creates dynamic conversations that reduce the knowing-doing gap within a school and eventually, within an entire school district. As grade-level teams and content- or course-specific teams find consensus on the essentials of the curriculum, the teams not only clarify learning expectations for their own students, they also support the work of *vertical* teams; they help chart the learning journey of students over time as they grow and pass through the school and district. Mapping promotes a living curriculum because it deals with real time. Teachers can actually "tell it like it is" rather than cope with a bureaucratic approach to describing the flow of their classrooms (Jacobs, 1997). The opportunity for teacher teams to share and develop common content and skills that support the essential questions linked to a specific curricular standard moves curriculum from a static, archived document to a dynamic and interactive system.

Making Sense of Assessment

As curriculum mapping and collaborative discussions facilitate clarity about what we want our students to know, they can also address the second critical question of a professional learning community: "How do we know that they have learned it?" (DuFour, DuFour, Eaker, & Many, 2006) To find the answer to this question, teams look at their everyday classroom assessment practices.

How can assessment enhance learning for all students? This critical question remains a priority as we discuss assessments and ponder how we can develop those assessments that actually enhance learning within the classroom. Since the late 1800s, talking about assessment has often meant talking about *grades*; we selected and sorted students based upon their scores to create winners and losers within our classrooms. This approach does give us some students who "get it" and move on to the next lesson, but we are just as likely to encounter students who struggle to learn and ultimately don't "get it." We know that these students can then become disengaged in school; they frequently create discipline problems within the classroom and fall further behind every year. They are potential school dropouts.

Since entering the 21st century, we have heard the plea to develop common assessments, investigate the results of the assessments, and make instructional decisions based upon the results. Teams of teachers throughout North American raced to complete these common assessments and to adjust our teaching. Often, however, the common assessment didn't eliminate the problems of a poorly designed classroom test, but rather increased the number of students subject to a poorly designed collaborative test. In many cases, we failed to investigate how these assessments were actually impacting the learning within our classrooms; we were simply creating additional student performance data to further validate the grades we assigned to students who didn't learn. Many have heard assessment expert Rick Stiggins say that when it comes to formative assessment, "It's not the type of assessment that counts, it's how the assessment is being used." The challenge is to create common assessments to guide our students through their learning process, rather than measurements to evaluate instruction. But all too often, rather than developing common formative assessments, we created an additional summative test for our students instead.

Research indicates that ongoing formative assessment significantly improves student learning, while summative assessments have limited effect upon student learning. In their review of the research, Paul Black and Dylan Wiliam (1998) found, in fact, that it is possible to enhance learning for all students on summative assessments by simply using ongoing formative assessments to adjust instruction. Rick Stiggins and his coauthors (2004) further expanded our understanding of effective assessment *for* learning (rather than *of* learning) by identifying five keys of high quality assessments. These keys can guide our consideration of best assessment practices in the classroom (Stiggins, Arter, Chappuis, & Chappuis, 2004). Asking critical questions about each of the five keys will help us create accurate assessments and use them effectively to further the learning of our students. The five keys are as follows:

Key 1: Clear Purpose—What is the purpose of our assessment, and who will benefit from the results of the assessment?

Key 2: Clear Targets—What is it that we are assessing, and what are the learning targets?

Key 3: Good Design—How are we assessing, and what is the proper method to assess the learning targets found in Key 2?

Key 4: Sound Communication—How are we communicating about the assessment, and how will we manage the information?

Key 5: Student Involvement—How do we involve students in the assessment process, and create an opportunities for students to understand the learning targets and how can students monitor their progress throughout their learning? (Stiggins, Arter, Chappuis, & Chappuis, 2004)

Each key provides a framework for a critical conversation about classroom assessment practice. The keys assist us in shifting the focus of our conversation from our teaching strategies to our students' learning.

Alignment of Curriculum Maps to Assessments for Learning

The data on our taught curriculum that we've recorded in our curriculum maps becomes essential as we enter the assessment conversation. Since curriculum maps are dynamic documents that provide evidence of actual classroom teaching, we can use maps to identify the actual learning targets located within our taught curriculum. By taking time to identify student learning targets in our maps, we clearly identify what we want our students to know and be able to do. Learning targets are identified by deconstructing state and local standards. This is not easy work. It is best accomplished by teams of teachers who collaborate on a course or grade-level subjects.

Once we identify learning targets, we must match them to the projection maps so that we increase the opportunity for learning around those targets. Without those standard drive targets to anchor our teaching and student learning, we may create powerful lessons around the wrong learning.

As we invite students to participate in the assessment process, it is vital that we develop clear learning targets (Key 2). Learning targets represent the knowledge and skills that students must attain, and students can't hit a target they can't see. Learning targets should parallel Bloom's Taxonomy, becoming gradually more complex to encourage higher-level thinking skills in our students (Stiggins, Arter, Chappuis, & Chappuis, 2004).

The base learning target is knowledge: "What is it we want our students to know?" We identify specific knowledge targets during collaborative conversations. Reasoning, the second learning target, occurs when students take the knowledge they have acquired and apply to it critical thinking and problem-solving skills. Reasoning leads to the development of the third level, skill targets. Skill targets identify the actions needed to implement knowledge and reasoning. When learning requires the creation of a tangible construct like a graph or a plan, we reach the fourth level of learning targets: products.

To clearly articulate to students what we want them to learn in relation to a particular standard, a teacher team must deconstruct the standard into specific learning targets at each level. Often the written standard does not reveal the critical information about what we actually want the student to learn. A deconstructed standard clearly identifying specific learning targets that is placed in the curriculum map actually guides the learning for both the student and teacher:

- What knowledge do we want students to know within this standard?

- What patterns of reasoning are essential to understand this standard?

- What skills are necessary?

- What products must students create to meet this standard?

Through powerful team consideration of these questions, we discover how more complex learning targets like skills and products are built upon knowledge and reasoning targets, and we define the critical learning that should take place within every classroom.

This is only the first step, however. Our collaborative team discussion now determines the curriculum content and assessments essential for the mastery of the identified targets. After deconstructing the standard into specific learning targets, the team should try to locate those targets in their curriculum maps to ensure that students are learning the written curriculum. Clarity about learning targets also facilitates the opportunity to discuss the best assessment for the target. It is very common to create an assessment measuring content and skills found within our standards. Rarely do we consider the specific targets of reasoning and products contained in our standards. If the standard contains all four learning targets (knowledge, reasoning, skills, and products), then we would classify the standard as a product standard. If the standard contains only knowledge targets, then it is simply a knowledge standard, and so on. The assessment should match the learning target identified by the standard.

During my tenure as a high school principal, I always knew exactly when the biology teachers were teaching a specific standard associated with cells. This standard read: *Students will demonstrate an understanding of the structure and function of a cell.* Every year during that unit, students would fill our hallways and biology classrooms with all types of cakes, popcorn balls, Jell-O molds—a variety of jiggling, edible globs that they thought resembled cells. They enjoyed it so much that they made additional edible structures to represent cell organelles or cell parts. However, if we read the science standard closely, we have to acknowledge that it does not call for the students to create a product. This standard requires the student to have knowledge of the parts of the cell and to be able to use reasoning ability to explain how the cell parts function together.

We are continually faced with this quandary when we deeply investigate our curriculum. As we have crucial mapping conversations around each standard, we can clearly identify the essential learning targets and evaluate the quality of our assessments of student proficiency toward those targets. In essence, curriculum mapping and assessment for learning enhance the learning process in a mutually beneficial way. Both processes focus our attention on what we want students to learn within a particular standard. Upon further investigation of the cell standard, for example, it was impossible to assess the knowledge and reasoning learning targets via the ever-popular Jell-O and cakes. A more powerful assessment strategy would allow students to demonstrate their critical thinking through selected response and extended written response (Stiggins, Arter, Chappuis, & Chappuis, 2004). The creation of the jiggling cell model was a classroom activity that tapped the creativity of a few students, but as an assessment, it completely missed the learning target embedded in the standard. All too often instructional practice replicates activities such as the cell model. These activities often engage our students but fall short of an effective assessment of the desired curriculum. The opportunity for collaborative teams to discuss the actual biology standard or curriculum reinforces our need to become clear about the specific learning targets that we want our students to learn. As we become clear about the desired learning targets, teachers can develop accurate and effective assessments to measure the learning of our students. Collaborative team conversations provide the vehicle for teams to align the taught curriculum with the written curriculum as they develop proper assessment methods. Alignment of curriculum, instruction, and assessment is a collaborative process and is our best hope to reduce needless activities found in some of our classrooms.

As we collaboratively develop curriculum maps that integrate the five keys of effective assessments with the deconstructed standards, our conversations become increasingly focused on the essentials of student learning. We can then explore strategies to enhance the effective use of assessment through communication and student involvement.

Clarity and Coherence

In *The New Meaning of Educational Change* (2001), author Michael Fullan states, "Solutions must come through the development of *shared meaning.* The interface between individual and collective meaning and action in everyday situations is where change stands or fails" (p. 9). The collaborative process of curriculum mapping builds our shared knowledge of the curriculum and the assessment process for our students. We learn to shift our conversational focus from classroom strategies to the content and skills associated with learning the standard.

Fullan further states, "This is not a race to see who can become the most innovative. The key words are meaning, coherence, connectedness, synergy, alignment and capacity for continuous improvement" (2001, p. 19). It is our challenge in our teams, schools, and districts to make these words part of our professional reality. We have to be clear on the meaning of student learning. We have to constantly strive for coherence and connectedness to our learning-focused practices so that our plates do not become overloaded. We must build synergy and alignment. All of these ideas help us build our individual and collective capacity for continuous school improvement.

The development of professional learning communities creates the best chance to create synergy and alignment of essential school improvement initiatives for improved student learning. Individual teachers and schools struggled to move these research-based initiatives (such as curriculum mapping and assessment for learning) through the classroom door for systemic school improvement. The collaborative process builds capacity for teachers to take the first step on their journey to become a learning-centered school versus a teacher-centered school. The first two questions of a PLC—"What do we want all students to know and be able to do?" and "How will we know students have learned?" (DuFour, DuFour, Eaker, & Many, 2006)—create a symbiotic relationship within the school improvement process. This chapter allows teams to consider a process to close the gap between the written and taught curriculum as they identify learning targets with properly aligned assessment methods that promote student learning. The threshold to our classrooms will open as teachers deprivatize their practice creating a pathway for critical conversations with an intense focus on student learning.

References

Black, P., & Wiliam, D. (1998, October). Inside the black box: Raising standards through classroom achievement. *Phi Delta Kappan, 80*(2), 139–148.

DuFour, R., DuFour, R., Eaker, R., & Many, T. (2006). *Learning by doing: A handbook for professional learning communities at work.* Bloomington, IN: Solution Tree.

DuFour, R., & Eaker, R. (1998). *Professional learning communities at work: Best practices for enhancing student achievement.* Bloomington, IN: Solution Tree (formerly National Educational Service).

Fullan, M. (2001). *The new meaning of educational change.* New York: Teachers College.

Jacobs, H. H. (1997). *Mapping the big picture: Integrating curriculum and assessment K–12.* Alexandria, VA: Association for Supervision and Curriculum Development.

Johnson, S. M., & Donaldson, M. (2007, September). Overcoming the obstacles to leadership: Teachers as leaders. *Educational Leadership, 65*(1), 8–13.

Marzano, R. (2003). *What works in schools: Translating research into action.* Alexandria, VA: Association for Supervision and Curriculum Development.

Pfeffer, J., & Sutton, R. (2000). *The knowing-doing gap: How smart companies turn knowledge into action.* Boston: Harvard Business School.

Stiggins, R., Arter, J., Chappuis, J., & Chappuis, S. (2004). *Classroom assessment for student learning: Using it right, doing it well.* Portland, OR: Assessment Training Institute.

Udelhofen, S. (2005). *Keys to curriculum mapping: Strategies and tools to make it work.* Thousand Oaks, CA: Corwin.

Part Three

USING DATA TO REACH ALL STUDENTS

LILLIE G. JESSIE

 Lillie Jessie has provided award-winning leadership throughout her 17-year tenure as principal of Elizabeth Vaughan Elementary School in Woodbridge, Virginia. Her innovative, proactive approach has raised the school to unprecedented levels of success. Locally recognized in 2003–2004 as a School of Excellence, Vaughan was honored in 2006 as one of 69 schools in Virginia to close the achievement gap between low- and middle-income students. The school also opened the first student-run bank in an elementary school in Prince William County Public Schools (PWCS), and received the performance-based PWCS Business Partnership Award. For achieving amazing goals using the Professional Learning Communities at Work process, Vaughan is one of eight schools featured in the video *The Power of Professional Learning Communities at Work: Bringing the Big Ideas to Life*. It is also listed as an evidence of effectiveness school on www.allthingsplc.info.

SEVEN

Teaching in the Dark

Lillie G. Jessie

I could never go back to teaching without the use of data. Teaching without data would be like getting dressed in the dark.

—Myesha Taylor, first-grade teacher

Myesha Taylor is just one of the many phenomenal teachers at Vaughan Elementary. Unfortunately, Myesha's view is not the view of every teacher in North America, or even every teacher at Vaughan. Many teachers are still "teaching in the dark" without using data, hoping to hit but often missing their critical target: high performance for all students. Our end-of-the-year test results should never be a surprise. For many teachers, however, this is still the case, because they have not moved from *hoping* for better results to *knowing* what to expect from children. Not only are we teaching in the dark, but we are blaming the poor results on our students.

Moving from hoping to knowing requires what we commonly refer to as "mirror check" in my school. Teachers reach a level of growth that allows them to establish personal barometers of high achievement for themselves and the students they serve. In order to do this, they understand and are willing to "expose" their "failures and weaknesses and . . . fears to another person" (Lencioni, 2002, p. 14). They know that accepting their own temporary failures is the precursor to high levels of success. They have also learned one of life's great lessons, which is the power and absolute necessity of collaboration.

I have been in the business of diagnostic prescriptive teaching and the use of data to determine the instructional needs of children for many years. During that period of time I have conducted a personal meta-analysis of sorts and drawn my own conclusions about the need for teachers to use some type of data analysis to guide their instruction. No, I have not conducted the longitudinal and cross-sectional analysis done by Robert Marzano and his colleagues, but I have observed firsthand the effects of using data—or not—to make critical daily instructional decisions in classrooms.

We began the data "sharing" journey at Vaughan as early as 1992, but we discovered that *sharing* data was not sufficient. We did not achieve accreditation for the State of Virginia Standards of Learning and School of Excellence until 2002, after we implemented a very important tenet of a PLC: *using* data to guide instruction. We then received additional national recognition for closing the achievement gap between minority and majority students. In 2007, when 55% of school divisions in Virginia and the state as a whole did not make adequate yearly progress, Vaughan did. The PLC process works, but it is teachers seeking and *implementing* strategies to achieve more for their students who make the difference.

In this chapter, we will walk through the developmental stages experienced when a staff learns to share data and use it to change their instruction. I have included observations from two colleagues who provide the perspectives of a teacher and an administrator. Antoinette McDonald is one of the most dedicated, creative, and insightful teachers I have had the pleasure of working with at Vaughan, and Rachel English is a retired principal who worked with me during my tenure as Title I Supervisor in the early 1970s, and as my assistant principal in the 1990s. We are kindred spirits in our thinking.

The professional learning community process by its very nature involves ups and downs along the way. Why? We have to change how we view children and our responsibility for their success in a radical way. When teachers shine a little light on their practices—by discussing data, engaging in collective inquiry, and involving students in data discussions and responses—they raise their own performance and that of their students. When we teach in the light of data, we move from *hoping* we look good when we showcase our performance to *knowing* we look good. There is beautiful light at the end of the PLC journey, with dancing and singing. At a PLC Summit in July, 2005, Andrea Phillips, another teacher at Vaughan, put it this way: "When we look in the mirror, we want to look good! We enjoy bragging about our accomplishments."

This wonderful end could happen for any school and any teacher. It does not have to take those of you reading this chapter as long as it took my school, because you have access to more information and successful projects to use as models. Rachel and I now realize that we were "data-driven" as early as 1970, but we were far from being a professional learning community back then. We collected data *of* learning, but not *for* learning (Stiggins, 2007). In other words, we did not use the data to guide instruction, only to fill out local and state-mandated accountability reports. During the 1990s, when Vaughan began its transformation, there was some but not a great deal of pressure for high performance on a national or local level. Teachers would say, "Other schools aren't doing this, so why are we?" Other teachers in our district felt sorry for Vaughan teachers because they worked for a lady who required them to read books! As educators it speaks badly of our profession when our colleagues avoid the very thing we penalize children for not doing—reading and learning.

I have concluded that there are stages of development before teachers voluntarily use data to guide instruction. Furthermore, there are reasons for their reluctance to "buy in" to this process. Early in my career as principal at Vaughan Elementary, for example, I introduced a process inspired by the book *Results* by Mike Schmoker (1996). In our business, we are experts at creating acronyms, and I was very proud of my acronym for our new process: DOD. It aligned so perfectly with our students, who are children of military personnel and federal government employees working in Washington, DC. To me, DOD stood for the Day of Dialogue, but teachers secretly called it Day of *Dread* or even the Day of *Death*. They felt these quarterly sharing days were done for my benefit alone and took away their valuable instructional time. Remember, according to Marzano's analysis (2007), instructional time can be as low as 21%, but only as high as 69%. Instructional time is always vulnerable, even under the best conditions. As I reflect on those early days, I must admit the teachers were right: The DOD *did* take away from instruction time, since some teachers didn't use the information gleaned there to change their instructional practices.

Although we lost instructional time, however, I am not convinced that we lost *learning* time. As you know, teachers hold themselves to a higher standard in a PLC environment, including a focus on learning and results (Schmoker, 2006). These quarterly sharings served as the beginning of our shift from teaching to learning. Persons participating in the early DOD process now see it as a necessary part of their growth in the PLC journey.

I have observed seven stages along the journey of buy-in to using data:

1. Shock

2. Professional resistance

3. Fear

4. Reluctant compliance

5. Discovery

6. Bargaining

7. Advocacy

This chapter will explore these stages. It is important to note that teachers in the same school may be at different stages of development. Veteran teachers may never have bought in to the need to use assessment to guide instruction, for example. Principals and teachers who sit on interview panels also know that there is that newly hired teacher, who said in the interview what he or she thought you wanted to hear about assessment, and then there is the real teacher, who "shows up" with very strong and opposing views on the use of assessment. These teachers may want to work with others, but like the teacher Peter Miller in Rick DuFour's epilogue in *Ahead of the Curve* (2007), they may find the job to be more than they bargained for. Over time, new teachers coming into a school may or may not embrace PLC principles. I have seen both.

The all-too-familiar term *professional learning community* has taken on real meaning during my tenure as a principal. Rick DuFour frequently reminds us that learning is embedded in a PLC—that we learn from each other. When Vaughan began on the unpopular and then-unmandated path of using data, some of us felt it was nonsensical to plan instruction without the use of data. Others felt it was a waste of time. So it was very fulfilling when I recently overheard a formerly reluctant teacher proudly say to a new teacher, "We've been using data at this school for years." Jonnah Douglas, a visiting international faculty member, after only a year in our school, was assisting in an interview for vacated position at her grade level, when to my surprise, she asked the applicant, "Are you willing to share data with others?" When the applicant gave a lukewarm response, she prodded: "Is that going to be a problem for you? You see, we work as a team in this school."

Teachers are like doctors, businessmen, and athletes. They want to be applauded and treated as professionals. They will embrace successful practices. I have learned not to confuse reluctance or resistance with total defiance: Questioning is part of the learning curve. It is *okay* to be at that stage. The important thing is to recognize and accept where you are and keep moving until you get to the "good stuff"—high levels of learning for your students. I've observed these stages of embracing the use of data over a long period of time. I hope they make you laugh out loud, as they do for me. We could use a little bit of levity in this very serious business!

Stage 1: Shock

"You have got to be kidding!"

Teacher Antoinette McDonald suggests that teachers at this stage feel that "teaching is enough. . . . I did not sign up for all of this other stuff, too." To them, the word *data* is not only scary, it is taboo. According to Rachel English, teachers at this stage are prone to reminding us that this requirement was "not a part of the original interview."

Very few, if any, questions about accountability for learning are part of the typical new teacher interview. We talk about discipline, parental involvement, teamwork, and instructional content, but we stay away from accountability. We are afraid that teachers will not accept the position if accountability became a requirement! Some teachers at this stage *do* avoid schools that require high degrees of accountability. They seek refuge in what Doug Reeves call the "lucky" schools: those with middle-class students who are already reading when they start school.

When you think about it, few, if any, other employment fields works like this. Rick Stiggins (2007) talks about students being unable to hit the learning target even when the target is *not* constantly shifting because we do not have a clear picture of what we want students to learn. The same is true for teachers. We interview teachers without telling them what we really want—accountability—then we require them to be accountable after they have signed the dotted line. After the initial interview, we move the target from teaching to learning, and in some instances, the teacher is the last to know.

One of the reasons principals are having this dilemma is our unwillingness to treat teachers like professionals and discuss what some have called the "nondiscussibles." Another nondiscussible is the simple issue of knowing what to teach. Some teachers are shocked when asked to defend their rationale for teaching an objective. The usual reason is, "The textbook tells us what to teach." We principals and central office give you a huge, unmanageable curriculum guide or a textbook—written by a stranger who knows nothing about your students—and say, "Go for it!" This scenario will continue until teachers and administrators acquire a higher level of confidence in our ability to make curriculum decisions related to the essential learning outcomes we seek. As early as 1970, Ron Edmonds, in his Effective Schools movement, said that we know all we need to know (Lezotte & McKee, 2002). We just need to find time to *share* what we know.

According to Robert Marzano (2003), a curriculum first must be viable before you can guarantee implementation: That is, it has to be manageable. Teachers come to me and say, "The curriculum notebook is too big." In essence, they are saying, "We don't know where to start." It becomes easier to use a textbook that, in their estimation, is at least manageable. But most of us know that in spite of their convenience, textbooks are rarely aligned with the local and state curriculum and are often written at too high a readability level. The only way to overcome this is to select the most important or "power" standards (Ainsworth, 2007) that are to be taught and assessed out of this maze of objectives. Taking responsibility for defining the content is no small task. No wonder some teachers react with shock!

Stage 2: Professional Resistance

"I don't have time for testing. . . . I've got to teach!"

I cannot tell you how many times I have heard teachers say this. But the question we have to ask ourselves is, "Teach what?" Imagine what would happen if doctors used the same logic and said, "I don't have time to look at those x-rays, I just need to operate."

We ask, "Teach what?" because too often we give our teachers testing instruments that do not provide information—data—to guide instruction. Sadly, the instruments lack content validity, reliability, or both. Even sadder, the teacher often receives the data too late to influence teaching decisions. We wouldn't want our doctor to receive our x-rays after surgery, or to receive an x-ray of our head when we're scheduled for open-heart surgery. Yet we do this on regular basis in this field. Steve Edwards, noted national consultant and author, visited our school. One teacher asked what he considered to be "too much testing." His response was profound: "One test is too much if it is not used to guide instruction."

The concern of time for instruction does have some validity, as discussed earlier. The solution is to provide time for teachers to discuss curriculum and assessment and determine those power standards discussed earlier. Teachers in my school found one instrument that had the alignment they were seeking, and now that assessment has been stored electronically for easy access. It provides preassessment, ongoing, simulated, and summative data. I learned something valuable from my staff: Teachers are not *opposed* to assessment. They are opposed to poorly aligned assessments! Teacher confidence in a measure is a prerequisite to its use. There is always time for the right assessment.

Stage 3: Fear

"Will my data be used against me?"

This stage speaks for itself. At Vaughan, public sharing of data is the norm—it's one of the tenets of a PLC. Antoinette says that this practice scared her to death when she was hired. Would poor test results be used to fire her or transfer her to a grade that she had not selected or desired?

In a professional learning community, principals and teachers see enough data from each team to learn that we always have strengths and weaknesses. We use our results not to punish, but as an opportunity to obtain reteaching help from our teammates. We rely on each other. Once we achieve this interdependence—which comes only with trust—teachers realize that they can best master the long lists of learning objectives by working in a collaborative manner. They begin to use data as opportunities to ask for help instead of opportunities to point fingers.

This does bring me to another important point. Rachel and I have had numerous discussions over the years about the fact that educators—teachers and principals—have to be held accountable in the same way as persons in other business fields. Sometimes the data suggests that poor instruction has taken place by an individual teacher on a substantial scale or over a long period of time. This is where the principal's moral purpose may collide with his or her desire to be popular. *Interdependence* as defined in a PLC does not mean teachers should carry the load for the ineffective practices of a colleague.

Interestingly enough, I have found that teachers themselves want principals to remove persons from their team who demonstrate continued unwillingness to become more effective. Teachers in PLC environments have a laser-like focus on the concept of "our" kids rather than "your" kids. Since the students belong to everyone, everyone is asked to perform—and is supported. Howard Gardner (2004) listed seven ways to change a person's thinking; the list runs from reason to confrontation. He reminds us that sometimes we must use the last resort; resistance must be confronted and dealt with. Rick DuFour (2004) agrees with Gardner's premise and reminds us that *how* we confront individuals is critical to our success; we must focus, he suggests, on the *behavior* displayed by the individual, not the attitude.

PLC teachers are sympathetic but will not tolerate lack of commitment or long-term ineffectiveness. If necessary, they will go to the principal for help.

Stage 4: Reluctant Compliance

"You can make me collect data, but you can't make me use it."

At this stage, a staff collects data, but only because the local or district administration demands a report. Rarely are the results used to guide instruction. The general feeling is, "I'm glad that's over. Now I can go back to teaching." I call this the "pretty paper" stage because reports full of beautiful graphs can camouflage our desire to maintain the status quo.

My teachers and I have seen this scary stage played out on a few occasions. The scary part is that the data presented can be misleading to the principal and to those depending on the teacher—the students. Sometimes in this new climate of accountability, or in schools where everyone seems to be chanting, "We are a PLC," a person can and will present data that he or she thinks the principal and the team want—instead of the real data. In a hurry to "get this off my plate" or "give them what they want," some teachers may present information that lacks precision and accuracy. This is where the norms of the group, collective responsibility, and level of trust discussed by Lencioni (2002) come in to play. Sometimes, a teacher in a high-performing team needs the reassurance of knowing that he or she does not have to be at the same high level of performance of her team members. Early in the norm-setting process, a team must establish a culture of acceptance: a culture of accepting each other's current and more importantly, *accurate* reality.

Teachers in our school quickly realized they could be involved in meaningless instruction if misleading data was presented. Results should never be a surprise, but if you or your teammates remain at the pretty paper stage, get ready for the nasty surprise ending when schoolwide test scores come back. One reason teachers may stall at this stage is overload. Dr. DuFour and others warn us that we can lose great programs because teachers and staff are too tired to listen. He frequently reminds us, "Listen deeply." Your responsibility as a teacher is to present your concerns in a professional manner instead of whispering them in the "teacher lounge of discontent." Most principals will listen to a formal expression of concern; principals *have* to listen to what teachers are saying.

Stage 5: Discovery

> *"My kids are learning more than I thought. . . . I can spend my time teaching other things."*

When you change your focus from teaching to learning, something *magical* happens. According to Antoinette, this is when the "light bulb of ownership first takes place. . . . Data becomes your friend." Or as Rachel puts it, this is when teachers realize that data is not going to be used for evaluation—that it is "safe" to show results that are not at the performance level of your colleagues. You think, "Maybe there's something to this PLC thing."

You begin to realize you've been missing out on one of the best-kept secrets and the greatest timesaving devices known to man: a map. Checking your map before heading to a destination can save you valuable time. For example, approximately 6 weeks before the administration of our Virginia Standards of Learning (SOL) test, my school gives tests that are similar to the SOLs in content, scope, and format. Teachers are amazed at what students have actually learned and retained when we see the results. Our curriculum plan for the remaining 6 weeks is based on facts rather than guesswork. Teachers see that they have gone from a pretest matrix that is a "sea of red" (which represents lack of mastery) to strips of red. They frequently say something like, "I could have wasted my time teaching skills that students didn't need."

Stage 6: Bargaining

> *"Something's in this for me after all. I am willing to teach this skill area for our entire grade level since my kids performed well, if you would be willing to work with my students during that period of time."*

It's human nature to ask, "What's in it for me?" This is the moving from "me" to "we" stage. At this stage, you begin to think of "our" kids instead of "your" kids. You now see where this PLC thing is going, and you even volunteer to teach a skill that your students mastered to other students in exchange for help from another teacher.

You are now beginning to realize the power of collaboration and interdependence in a PLC environment. You realize that you don't have to do everything alone—that it is okay to not be good at teaching every objective in the curriculum. Lack of success on a given date is only temporary, if the next step is to find a solution. We often talk about students needing second chances; teachers need second chances, too. One principal asked me, "How do you get your teachers to publicly share data?" After some thought, I said, "They know that it is not a final judgment." Public sharing affirms your skills as professionals. It also affords the opportunity to ask for help.

We had several staff members leave unexpectedly in 2006 due to medical or personal reasons. Teachers were so concerned about our kids that they volunteered to assume teaching roles for their missing colleagues' students. It never entered their minds that a substitute would teach "our" kids; they preferred to take on larger classrooms themselves. In spite of all of this, we still made AYP, a problem for our school division and the state of Virginia. We absolutely would *not* have made AYP had it not been for the PLC process in our school. One new teacher outlined what would have happened at her former school:

- Fellow teachers would have had no idea where the absent teacher's students were in relation to the curriculum.

- There would be no data to guide any replacement instruction.

- The remaining teachers would not have had the trust to pull together.

- No one would have even thought to take in the extra students.

She summed up how teachers in her old school would have responded: "We would have thought, 'Too bad, hope they make it,'" she said, "then closed our doors, and continued to teach our *personal* classes."

Stage 7: Advocacy

> *"I can't live without data! Teaching without data is like dressing in the dark."*

This is the ultimate stage that you want to reach in a PLC environment. Remember, though, at the beginning of this chapter, I warned you that everyone will not be at the same stage of development. I operate on the concept of "catch the wave." Somewhere in the Effective Schools research, there was the observation that one or two teachers wanting to embrace effective school practice cannot survive in a school full of naysayers. The same is true in a school of believers: Naysayers cannot survive when surrounded by positive forces. The difference between teachers at this stage versus the other stages is that they become *advocates*!

As teachers at this stage, your advocacy will be shared with others in many forums, including learning celebrations. If there is a pep rally, you become the organizer, not the principal. Yes, there can be a stage 4 (Reluctant Compliance) teacher in midst of a celebration of success. For a long time, many of my teachers would not display pride in their students' performance. Like their attitude toward data, their attitude about pom poms was, "You can make me hold them, but you can't make me shake them!" I cannot tell you how many times I have heard teachers say, "We have to get students ready for the real world," or "We don't want them to have too much fun at this pep rally because they will be hyper when they return to class." Teachers at the advocacy stage know that student efficacy is critical to high performance. They know that their students are just like them: *They can't live without* the immediate feedback of data.

You don't need a meta-analysis to see how feedback works. Watch the crowd at any football game, and you'll know that the level of excitement about the game is feedback based on what's happening right then on the field. That's why we have instant replay; we want more detailed feedback. That is also why there is such a thing as "home field advantage." The players not only have the playbook and know the landscape, but they also have the advantage of cheering fan feedback. There is no difference inside the school building. You and your students both need to have the home field advantage. Both of you need access to the playbook and its data on all the plays that worked and those that didn't. More importantly, students need you, their teacher, as the coach, providing them with play-by-play instructions. You cannot be the coach in a classroom if you do not have data in your playbook.

How do students and teachers "look" at this last stage? They certainly do not look like they got dressed in the dark. In the world of sports, the dress is preselected; every detail of the uniform is considered before the players leave the locker room. Coaches know that the way a person looks and feels about himself is critical to his success. That is why they clothe players with belief and information before entering the arena. In most games, there are many second chances before the game is over. In football, you get four chances to make a first down. Students deserve second chances—second chances supported with new approaches that will make them successful. Having data in your playbook is the only way that goal can be achieved.

Steps for Moving From Shock to Advocacy

Reality Checks

The first and most important element in making a transition between stages is to recognize and accept where you are on this data-use continuum. I find this to be one of the most challenging aspects of this business. I cannot tell you how many times I have heard or seen educators point the finger at others, asking them to change when in fact they are the ones who need to change. The need to accept your current reality and respond to the brutal facts permeates the presentations by Rick DuFour, Becky DuFour, and Bob Eaker because they know that this is the essential foundation for a PLC.

Acceptance and Support for Colleagues

There are reasons people are and remain at the lowest level (shock) of this continuum. These observations are supported by the research of Douglas Reeves (2006) in his book *The Learning Leader.* There he describes "lucky" schools and "losing" schools; both place little emphasis on change or school improvement, but for two very different reasons. Lucky schools have middle-class majority populations; students there pass the minimal standards with minimal intervention. Teachers there feel little reason to change when they enter another environment or when a new leader seeks higher performance. Losing schools with high-minority, low-income student populations, on the other hand, often have low expectations of students compounded by a "blame the victim" mentality. Teachers from both of these schools need time and support as they get over the shock of being accountable for *learning*. Prior to entering your arena, they were only accountable for *teaching*.

Scheduling

Teachers demand time for lesson planning but fail to seek the same amount of time for data analysis. The latter is a prerequisite to effective planning; make it a priority. My school provides the weekly planning time and also provides teachers with selected days of substitute coverage to prepare for our data-sharing sessions. It is on our master calendar, which is prepared by a teacher committee. The money spent for substitute coverage on these days is the wisest investment a principal can make.

Be prepared for some *needed* conflict when you engage in this task. Reaching consensus on the yearly calendar of time needed for each grade level or program is difficult but critical. I have found that it takes an entire day at a minimum. I have also found that it is best that the principal *not* enter the room!

Dispersed Leadership

Educators at various stages of this continuum are present within every school, grade, and department. One individual may be at the "shock" level while others in the same group are at higher levels. Colleagues at the advocacy stage can serve as mentors and support others. For example, we have found one person who acts as a Data Lead for each grade level and instructional team. There seems to always be one person who loves numbers and data, and another who is the peacekeeper or climate-watcher.

Assign roles to all members of the team during the actual data-sharing forums. The person who acts as the master of ceremonies for our data luncheons, Shirley Bunch, is not a teacher but our media specialist. Why? Because she is good at it! Allowing people to do what they enjoy or what they are good at doing is *what a PLC is all about*. This sense of interdependence and support from others makes the transition to a higher level easier.

Student Efficacy

Include students in data sharing and accountability for learning. Teachers and students become very territorial when they are asked to share data, test-taking strategies, and excitement for learning. They do what the famous chef Emeril advocates on his cooking show—they "kick it up a notch." It creates a little subtle competition, and it is *fun!*

Teacher Confidence in the Assessment

Pivotal to our success was teacher confidence in the required assessment by the school division. We know that there is confidence in common assessments developed by teachers, but there is a reality that we need to deal with in this business, and that is those assessments that are *required* by local school divisions. We found that we needed information from multiple assessments, including the one provided by our school division, but we have been allowed to use one that simulates the actual SOLs. Teachers in my school *cannot* and *will not* live without this vital assessment. As indicated earlier, teachers are not always opposed to testing; they are more opposed to *time-wasting* instruments that lack content validity and immediate and useful feedback.

Deprivatization of Practices

Data-sharing forums are the most powerful tools in developing data leaders (in a process the DuFours frequently refer to as *deprivatization*). At a principals' data forum, we were asked to share data collection strategies. While many shared how information was *sent* to their offices, I realized that there was something very unique about data sharing in a PLC environment: In a PLC, administrators *attend* the teachers' data-sharing meeting.

Teacher-controlled agendas are a prerequisite to teacher buy-in. When you teachers become advocates, you assume a leadership role. One way of achieving this leadership is to "invite" the principal to your grade level to share your accomplishments. The difference between data chats in a traditional environment and a PLC environment in my estimation is that in the former, we *share* data, but in the latter, we *respond* to data. The data-sharing template may vary, but it should have both sharing and responding components. Our template for weekly data meetings uses a version of the four critical questions of a PLC:

- Are the children learning?

- How do you know?

- What are your plans for those not learning?

- What are your plans for those who have mastered the essential questions?

Celebration of Success

On Gardner's (2004) lists of seven factors to change people's thinking, Resources and Rewards are number five. Attitudes and participation changed when we created public forums that allowed grade levels not only to celebrate their successes with the entire staff, but also to seek support from their colleagues. If you truly want to become a PLC, teachers have to know that it is okay to ask for help.

At Vaughan, we call the end-of-year data-sharing session a "brag" session. The quote on the agenda is: "Toot your own horn, or it will remain in a state of untootedness." You may have seen all of the hoopla that takes place at Vaughan in the video *The Power of Professional Learning Communities at Work*. What you didn't see is the day, once a year, when we leave the campus and go to a restaurant to eat on plates instead of trays, on tables covered in linen instead of plastic. As DuFour and Eaker say (quoting Terance Deal), without celebrations, every day of the week becomes an endless Wednesday (DuFour & Eaker, 1998). Teachers in a professional learning community should be treated like *professionals.*

At our celebration, *everyone* making a presentation receives a personal certificate of participation. Why? Because in a professional learning community, everyone is important to our shared success. Everyone has a light to shine into the dark.

Acknowledgments

I would like to thank the teachers at Vaughan Elementary who provided the insight for this chapter. Special thanks to my friend and colleague Rachel English who consulted with me and reminded me of the many professional experiences we shared during our more than 30 years of educational experience.

References

Ainsworth, L. (2007). Common formative assessments: The centerpiece of an integrated standards-based assessment system. In D. Reeves (Ed.), *Ahead of the curve: The power of assessment to transform teaching and learning* (pp. 79–101). Bloomington, IN: Solution Tree.

DuFour, R., & Eaker, R. (1998). *Professional learning communities at work: Best practices for enhancing student achievement.* Bloomington, IN: Solution Tree (formerly National Educational Service).

DuFour, R. (1998). Why celebrate? It sends a vivid message about what we value. *Journal of Staff Development, 19*(4), 58–59.

DuFour, R. (2004). Leading edge: Culture shift doesn't occur overnight and without change conflict. *Journal of Staff Development, 25*(4), 63–64.

DuFour, R. (2007). Once upon a time: A tale of excellence in assessment. In D. Reeves (Ed.), *Ahead of the curve: The power of assessment to transform teaching and learning* (pp. 253–267). Bloomington, IN: Solution Tree.

DuFour, R., Eaker, R., & DuFour, R. (Eds.). (2005). *On common ground: The power of professional learning communities at work.* Bloomington, IN: Solution Tree

DuFour, R., Eaker, R., & DuFour, R. (2007). *The power of professional learning communities at work: Bringing the big ideas to life* [Video]. Bloomington, IN: Solution Tree.

Fullan, M. (2006). Professional learning communities writ large. In R. DuFour, R. Eaker, & R. DuFour (Eds.), *On common ground: The power of professional learning communities* (pp. 209–223). Bloomington, IN: Solution Tree

Gardner, H. (2004). *Changing minds: The art and science of changing our own and other peoples' minds.* Boston: Harvard Business School.

Lencioni, P. (2002). *The five dysfunctions of a team: A leadership fable.* San Francisco: Jossey-Bass.

Lezotte, L., & McKee, K. (2002). *Assembly required: A continuous school improvement system.* Portland, OR: Educational Testing Service.

Marzano, R. (2003). *What works in schools: Translating research into action.* Alexandria, VA: Association for Supervision and Curriculum Development.

Marzano, R. (2007). Designing a comprehensive approach to classroom assessment. In D. Reeves, (Ed.), *Ahead of the curve: The power of assessment to transform teaching and learning* (pp. 103–125). Bloomington, IN: Solution Tree.

Reeves, D. (2006). *The learning leader: How to focus school improvement for better results.* Alexandria, VA: Association for Supervision and Curriculum Development.

Schmoker, M. (1996). *Results: The key to continuous improvement.* Alexandria, VA: Association for Supervision and Curriculum Development.

Schmoker, M. (2006). *Results now: How we can achieve unprecedented improvements in teaching and learning.* Alexandria, VA: Association for Supervision and Curriculum Development.

Stiggins, R. (2007). Assessment *for* learning: An essential foundation of productive instruction. In D. Reeves, (Ed.), *Ahead of the curve: The power of assessment to transform teaching and learning* (pp. 59–76). Bloomington, IN: Solution Tree.

AINSLEY B. ROSE

Ainsley Rose is the former director of education and curriculum for the Western Quebec School Board in Gatineau, Quebec. As an education leader, he incorporates his expertise in a wide range of principles, practices, and concepts that have been proven to improve schools, including Effective Schools, Professional Learning Communities at Work, instructional intelligence, and standards and assessment. Ainsley is trained in Stephen Covey's Seven Habits of Highly Effective People® and the TRIBES teaching process. He also conducts peer mediation for schools and has presented at the International Effective Schools Conference. He has served as chair of the Committee for Anglophone Curriculum Responsables and the Implementation Design Committee, and was named to the Advisory Board of English Education by the Minister of Education of Quebec. Ainsley has also received the Outstanding Achievement Award from the Association of Administrators of English Schools of Quebec.

EIGHT

Common Assessments: Bridging the Gap Between Teaching and Learning

Ainsley B. Rose

The teaching profession is a calling, a calling with the potential to do enormous good for students. Although we haven't traditionally seen it in this light, assessment plays an indispensable role in fulfilling our calling. Used with skill, assessment can motivate the unmotivated, restore the desire to learn, and encourage students to keep learning, and it can actually create—not simply measure—increased achievement.

—Rick Stiggins, Judith Arter, Steve Chappuis, & Jan Chappuis

Professional learning communities are driven by four key questions:

1. What do we want students to learn?

2. How will we know when they have learned?

3. How will we respond when they don't learn?

4. How will we respond if they have already learned it? (DuFour, DuFour, Eaker, & Many, 2006)

The development of common formative assessments is an essential process that influences so much of what teachers do on a daily basis to explore these questions. In order to achieve high levels of learning for all students, teachers must share a common basis for answering these questions. Common assessments—built by assessment-literate teachers and collaboratively scored using rubrics developed around provincial or state standards and outcomes—will provide this shared foundation (DuFour, DuFour, Eaker, & Many, 2006). Research has shown that when teachers develop common formative assessments, examine the results of these assessments in collaborative scoring sessions, and adjust instruction in light of the results of those common assessments, we *can* improve student achievement (Marzano, 2006).

This chapter will begin by addressing common questions about common assessments, shift to describing what processes are effective in developing and implementing common formative assessments in our schools, and finally will conclude by showing how the results from common assessments can inform teachers about what to change in their instructional repertoire.

Answering Common Questions on Common Assessments

All teachers within a professional learning community need to have shared understanding of the following questions (Stiggins, 2007):

- What do we mean by *common*?
- What data should we collect?
- How will the data inform instructional decisions?
- Who will make the critical decisions about student learning?
- How do we involve students in the assessment process?

So let's set about to answer these questions, as they are pivotal to the work of a PLC.

What Do We Mean by Common?

> [Common formative assessments are] assessments collaboratively designed by a grade-level or department team that are

administered to students by each participating teacher period-
ically throughout the year. They assess student understanding
of the particular standards that the grade-level or depart-
ment educators are currently focusing on in their individual
instructional programs. The teachers collaboratively score the
assessment, analyze the results and discuss ways to achieve
improvements in student learning on the next common for-
mative assessment they will administer.

—Larry Ainsworth & Donald Viegut

Common formative assessments are often thought of as periodic or interim assessments, collaboratively designed by grade-level or course teams of teachers, and administered to all students in a grade level or course several times during the quarter, semester, trimester, or entire school year. Designed as matching pre- and postassessments to ensure same-assessment to same-assessment comparisons, they are similar in design and format to district and state or provincial assessments (Ainsworth, 2007), but they are intended to provide information for immediate feedback while the learning is still taking place—that is, they are formative rather than summative.

Teachers may not be aware that much of what they do in the classroom constitutes the essence of formative assessment. Wiggins and McTighe (2007) emphasize the importance of ongoing classroom assessment that uses "a range of formal and informal methods such as quizzes, oral questioning, observations, draft work, think-alouds, student constructed concept maps, dress rehearsals, peer-response groups, learning logs and portfolio reviews" (p. 102). However, we must strive to go beyond that to create *common* formative assessments; common assessments provide the grist for collaborative discussions—the essence of the collaborative work of professional learning communities.

Teachers often raise concerns that they will lose professional independence if everything they do is expected to be in common with others. Rick DuFour (2006) notes, "Richard Elmore (2006, [p. 38]) wrote, 'Teachers have to feel that there is some compelling reason for them to practice differently, with the best direct evidence being that students learn better.'" Using common assessments does not in any way mean using *only* common assessments. In a PLC, common assessments may occur as frequently as three to four times a term, and discussion must follow each assessment, but teachers are still responsible for the day-to-day and minute-by-minute classroom feedback process for their own students.

Why should we consider common formative assessment as an essential part of the evaluation repertoire for teachers? Robert Marzano (2000) suggests that our present isolated assessment and grading practices are woefully antiquated and lead to three problems. Not doing common assessments allows teachers to "(1) include at their own discretion, different nonachievement factors in the assignment of grades; (2) it allows individual teachers to differentially weight assessment; and (3) it mixes different types of knowledge and skills into single scores on assessments" (Marzano, 2000, p. 13). All these then will have a profound impact on the accuracy of student achievement scores and the resulting decisions.

For example, there is often no clear policy in schools, let alone school districts, about how a grade on a report card is derived. Should it contain a combination of student tests results, participation in class, homework completion, behavior, and attitude? Are these weighted equally or not? Which of these might one categorize as "nonachievement" factors? Teachers often unknowingly give more weight to certain assessments than peers who teach the same subject at the same level. Indeed, there are many examples of different teachers grading the same student paper and arriving at a different result. In addition, a single score on an exam does not reveal the true result of student performance if the exam tests a range of skills or competencies, as most do. If two or more students receive the same score on such an exam, how can we be sure that we know each student's specific ability on each standard, skill, or competency tested? We cannot possibly compare assessment results if these types of discrepancies exist. Furthermore, not only can't we compare assessment results, but we can't provide equity in educational experience for students. Think about the ramifications of such discrepancies when we use these same marks to make decisions about honor rolls, eligibility for scholarships, entry to university, and other matters that have serious consequences for students' futures.

What Data Should We Collect?

In education we assess for two reasons: (1) to gather evidence of student achievement to inform instructional decisions and (2) to motivate learning. Virtually all school improvement models contend that schools will become more effective if the right people have access to the right evidence analyzed in the right way and used to inform the right decisions.

—Rick Stiggins

When we are clear about the learning targets we want students to reach, the most useful data allows us to give students timely, specific, descriptive, and frequent feedback as well as explicit instruction about the strategies, skills, and tactics that will lead students to gains in motivation and achievement. Furthermore, this data informs teachers about what they need to do to alter their instruction.

This was made all the more relevant on www.allthingsplc.info, a website and blog devoted to professional learning communities, in a posting that questioned whether "common assessments will limit us to a narrow focus on lower level skills." In response, Rick DuFour (2007) suggested we ask ourselves the following six questions about common assessments to determine their value and effect on student learning:

1. Do they help our team to identify students who are experiencing difficulty in their learning?

2. Do we have a plan in place to provide those students with additional time and support for learning?

3. Do we provide students with another opportunity to demonstrate their learning once they have been required to devote additional time to learning the skill or concept?

4. Do the results provide me with useful information as a teacher, helping me to identify areas where my students are not doing well compared with similar students pursuing the same curriculum?

5. Does student success on our common assessments translate into success on other high-stakes assessments such as state and national exams?

The answers to these questions most assuredly provide essential information. Not only will this information be useful to students, the primary users of assessment information, but also to teachers, who need to understand the effects of their instruction on student achievement and make decisions that will lead to higher levels of student motivation and success.

What Decisions Are Made Based on Assessment Data?

The critical instructional decisions made on the basis of common assessment results include:

- Whether a learning target or outcome has been achieved

- Which students require additional time and support

- Which areas require additional teaching

- Whether students will be ready for the summative assessment of learning at the end of the unit or course

- Whether curriculum is aligned across the grade or subject

- Whether teachers can employ effective strategies in their instruction in the event that one or more teachers are not obtaining satisfactory results

Giving parents a clear idea of how their child is progressing is another important consideration for the use of assessment data.

If we are engaged in common *summative* assessments, we may have an idea about whether students have met graduation requirements or need additional time at a grade level; where students who transfer to another school during or at the end of a school year should be placed academically; and which students are eligible for college or university entrance. These latter considerations result from a different type of assessment, but nevertheless serve to inform teachers, administrators, students, and their parents about progress toward targets or outcomes—all the more reason for consistency between and among teachers of similar grades and subjects.

Who Will Make the Critical Decisions About Student Learning?

> We must constantly remind ourselves that the ultimate purpose of assessment is to create autonomous students who are self-analyzing, self-evaluating, self-referencing, self-renewing, and self-motivating. This requires that students develop internal feedback spirals as a means of setting goals, planning actions, gathering data about their actions, reflecting on their own values, and altering their behaviors and values accordingly.
>
> —Art Costa & Bena Kallick

Teachers and administrators make some critical decisions about student learning; parents do as well, but to a lesser extent. While regular classroom formative assessment can provide both students and teachers with information they need, *common* formative assessments are much more meaningful. Common formative assessments are derived from collaborative examination of essential learnings and thus are aligned to end-of-term expectations. Collaboratively scored, their results can be used to align the curriculum. They drive individual teachers to learn effective practices that will lead them to similar success where their colleagues' classes may have performed more favorably. Teacher teams can monitor curriculum pacing to ensure that no students are at a disadvantage when the final assessment of learning takes place. Ultimately, as Ainsworth and Viegut (2006) point out, "For any educational improvement to bring about lasting change, classroom teachers must be provided the opportunity for significant investment and ownership in that improvement effort" (p. 4). I would add that to have even greater impact, this investment and decision-making must be collaborative.

The most important decisions about student learning, however, are those that students make for themselves. Sadler (1998) argues that we must make students aware of what the learning targets or goals are, where they are relative to those targets or goals, and what they must do to close the gap in their performance. Students who have information from common assessments about their strengths and weaknesses can set learning goals and gain an understanding about quality of work and effort required to meet those goals. Anne Davies (2000) emphasizes the importance of student involvement when she says, "As students participate in the assessment cycle they learn to become partners in the continuous assessment cycle. In this cycle students talk about what needs to be learned, set criteria and receive and give themselves descriptive feedback. From time to time they self assess and set goals" (p. 3). As a result, students become active partners in the learning process.

In support of the notion that students themselves play a pivotal role in taking responsibility for making decisions for their own learning, there are three skills that teachers can encourage in their students (Senge, McCabe, Lucas, Smith, Dutton, & Kleiner, 2000):

1. Self-management

2. Self-evaluation

3. Self-adaptation

The following questions define these skills.

> Self-management: How can students plan and organize their own learning? How can they set their goals, and name the milestones they expect to reach along the way?
>
> Self-evaluation: How can students evaluate and critique their own work? How can they critique the work of their peers and reflect on the differences in perception?
>
> Self-adaptation: How can students modify their working methods, based on the feedback they receive? How can they best be prepared to learn? (Senge et al., 2000, p. 191)

One often hears about the need to involve students in reflective activities as well as how assessment must inform instruction. What is not often stated, however, is that teachers should *model* these reflective behaviors with respect to their teaching practice. In a professional learning community, structured discussions focused on student achievement data create the circumstances for this reflection. If the results are not what were hoped for, teachers must reconsider Senge's questions and make decisions on ways to change their instruction to improve student learning.

How Do We Involve Students in the Assessment Process?

Stiggins, Arter, Chappuis, and Chappuis (2004) help us answer this question by identifying five steps by which students demonstrate involvement. Students involved in the assessment and learning process:

1. Understand learning targets.

2. Engage in self-assessment.

3. Watch themselves grow.

4. Talk about their growth.

5. Plan next steps.

Sadler (1989) adds that students should know what high-quality work looks like, be able to objectively compare their work to the standard, and have a store of tactics to make work better based on their observations. Among others, Black and Wiliam (1998), Davies (2000), Hattie (1992), and Marzano (2006) also argue that students must be involved in communicating about their learning, record-keeping, and participating in the assessment process.

But how do we involve students in the mechanics of the process, and at the same time engage their interest in taking ownership of their learning? One of the keys to involving students lies in the extent and frequency of which we provide feedback—as well as the type of the feedback we give. What we have come to learn is that not all feedback is created equal. Marzano's work (2006) distinguishes between encouraging and discouraging feedback and reveals the positive and negative effects both have on students as learners. Encouraging feedback "includes telling students what they have done well (positive reinforcement), and what they need to do to improve (corrective work, targets, etc.), but it also includes clarifying goals. The feedback must be informative rather than evaluative" (Hattie, 1992, as cited in Marzano, 2006, p. 5).

All feedback, whether common or not, whether positive or not, has some effect on student performance. The challenge is the extent to which students see the feedback as helpful and hopeful—whether the feedback encourages students to want to try again. If we rely solely on giving students numerical feedback—without explaining how the mark was derived or providing helpful suggestions about what they got wrong and what they might do about fixing it—our feedback merely makes a judgment about their worth and accomplishes little else. Surely there is little to be gained by only telling students how poorly they are doing. Feeling bad about doing poorly is no motivator to improve.

Ruth Butler's research (1988) frames this difference between informative and evaluative feedback as the difference between task-involving and ego-involving feedback. Comments are *task*-involving; marks or grades are *ego*-involving; feedback must be task-involving rather than ego-involving if it is to enhance achievement. Interestingly, comments given along with a mark have the same effect as marks alone—in other words, the value of comments is lost once a mark is assigned. In so far as the awarding of marks has the effect of stopping learning for many students, we must take full advantage of the benefits of formative assessment, which is characterized by written, descriptive, and task-involving feedback. This type of feedback is normally the domain of the classroom teacher and occurs daily, if not more frequently. However, the results from *common* formative assessments that are collaboratively scored and analyzed with appropriate feedback to students will result in greater beneficial impact on student learning than other assessments *of* learning that are distant from the classroom and occur only *occasionally*. Timely, specific, and descriptive feedback derived from collaboratively scored common formative assessments provide fair and accurate results about each student's proficiency level relative to the standards and end-of-year expectations.

Creating Common Assessments

If we can agree the evidence is compelling for schools to focus on the creation of common formative assessments, then the question becomes, "What must we do to ensure that schools and teachers become effective in creating high-quality common formative assessments, the results of which will be the driving force to change the instructional practices of individual teachers in order to raise student achievement levels for all students?" Up to this point I have outlined the compelling need to create common formative assessments and encouraged the foundational structure that brings together the alignment of curriculum with appropriate assessments. Therefore, it may be helpful at this point to outline the specific steps in the development of a common assessment. A more complete description of the entire process from development to data analysis can be found in the exemplary work of Larry Ainsworth and Donald Viegut in their book *Common Formative Assessments: How to Connect Standards-Based Instruction and Assessment* (2006). We must bear in mind that there are group behaviors that must be in place for any work to be effective and produce results; this discussion will emphasize the assessment design process rather than the characteristics of an effective team.

What, then, are the steps teachers, working in teams, should take to begin the design process? Most of the literature in this field suggests that we begin with a small pilot team of interested teachers and administrators from a school or district. Teams can include all teachers of same grade, same subject, same school, or even the district, particularly when there may only be one teacher in any given level or subject in a school.

To illustrate, let us assume that teachers from Typical Elementary School have volunteered to develop their first common formative assessment in grade 5 social studies. They meet and establish norms for guiding the work of the team. Whether or not those who are meeting have assessment expertise is not as important as beginning the process, because it is in the "doing" that collaborative teams learn what they need to be successful. In time, the need to create high-quality assessments will become the focus of the work of the team.

Stage One: Identify Essential Learning

In stage one of designing a common assessment, the team discusses the essential learning that is expected for its subject or grade level. Not all assessments are expected to measure all the outcomes at the same time, but the scope and sequence of those learning outcomes must align with what has been determined to be essential understanding in grade 5 social studies at Typical Elementary School. We must know the answer to "What do we want students to learn?" before we can create assessments to determine if they've learned it.

Stage Two: Assemble and Review Test Items

In stage two, the team conducts a review of potential test items. Team members determine the extent to which the test items match the specific standards that have been determined to be essential. Are some missing? Are too many being tested? Is there a fair distribution of standards being assessed? They then ensure that the test items are of high quality and that they will be measuring according to the appropriate method, as not all methods are as effective as others, depending on the outcomes being assessed (Stiggins et al., 2004). For example, selected response (multiple choice) is not always the most effective method to measure reasoning skills, nor is constructed response the most effective strategy to determine a performance standard.

Ainsworth and Viegut (2006) suggest these questions be asked:

1. Which types of assessment (multiple choice, selected response, and so on) did we include?

2. Which other types might we consider using?

3. Which standards would be best addressed by selected response or constructed response? (Essay or performance questions might also be appropriate.)

4. Will our assessment types provide us with a variety of evidence of our target learning or essential understanding?

5. What changes must we make to have alignment of all these goals of our common assessment?

Teams should examine the common formative assessment in its final form before the test is administered to students to ensure the quality of the assessment tool.

Stage Three: Design a Scoring Tool

In stage three, the collaborative team agrees on the evaluative criteria to determine proficiency, quality of response, and result or impact of the response. Rubrics are the most effective method of capturing all the elements for this phase of the design process. Rubrics are an essential tool in a standards-based approach to assessing the results of a common formative assessment. They allow the teachers to score the assessment according to agreed-upon guidelines in order to ensure consistency and avoid bias. Rubrics are essentially an evaluation tool with a fixed scale (either four, five, or six levels) that set out to describe different levels of performance, which teachers use to judge the level of performance or the degree of understanding that the student has demonstrated. Common rubrics, as with common assessment, serve to clarify what is to be learned and what the quality of student work should look like. These rubrics help both teachers as well as students in clarifying outcomes and quality in learning. As Wiggins and McTighe (2007) note, "Educators who have worked in teams to score student work often observe that the very process of evaluating student work against a common rubric teaches them a great deal about what make the products and performances successful" (p. 94).

Protocols are another effective, structured method of arriving at a common understanding in a collegial professional dialogue about student or teacher learning. For a more in-depth understanding of these procedures, refer to the original work from the Coalition of Essential Schools done by Joseph McDonald and David Allen (as cited in Blythe, Allen, & Powell, 1999; Wiggins and McTighe, 1998, 2005).

Stage Four: "Anchor" the Work

Once the actual assessment is administered to the various class-rooms, the final stage of the process is to reconvene the collaborative teams to review the student work and describe it (rather than grade it), according to the rubric designed for that purpose (see Ainsworth & Viegut, 2006, for more detail on describing rather than grading). Teachers first "anchor" the work resulting from the test by applying the criteria of each level on a rubric to various samples. The anchoring process requires that teachers sort the student work into groups of low-, medium-, and high-quality responses before scoring them independently. Once the rubric has been tested and consensus reached on scoring, the teams can score all the tests.

Using Common Assessment Results

> *Assessment is the process of gathering and discussing information from multiple and diverse sources in order to develop a deep understanding of what students know, understand, and can do with their knowledge as a result of their educational experiences.* **The process culminates when assessment results are used to improve subsequent learning.**
>
> —Teaching Effectiveness Program (emphasis added)

One of the most overlooked and understated aspects of the common formative assessment process and the role these assessments play in a professional learning community is the degree to which the results of high-quality assessments—of and for learning—inform teachers about how to change their instructional practice.

In their highly acclaimed article "Inside the Black Box," Black and Wiliam (1998, p. 138) point out, "Learning is driven by what teachers and pupils do in classrooms. Teachers have to manage complicated and demanding situations, channeling the personal, emotional, and social pressures of a group of 30 or more youngsters in order to help them learn immediately and become better learners in the future." Student achievement will meet the high expectations of the standards movement only if teachers can tackle this work more effectively. Increasing evidence shows that for any innovation to occur, there must be a fundamental shift in teaching practices in individual classrooms (Bennett & Rolheiser, 2001). This fact was also recognized in the TIMSS video study: "A focus on standards and accountability that ignores the processes of teaching and learning in classrooms will not provide the direction that teachers need in their quest to improve" (as cited in Black & Wiliam, 1998, p. 140).

Common assessment is among the many strategies, skills, and tactics available to teachers to improve the learning process for students. But do we have sufficient understanding of the integration of common formative assessment into the instructional process to use assessment results to clearly inform the next steps in helping students achieve at higher levels?

In order for teachers to adjust their instruction based on common assessment results, they must have a repertoire of instructional strategies, skills, and tactics to address specific student needs. We cannot leave to chance the proper instructional method that will elicit greater learning gains for the individual student. For example, how teachers structure groups in a cooperative lesson or how they might frame questions are highly technical aspects of their work in the classroom. Bennett and Rolheiser (2001) suggest, "The more deeply teachers understand instructional organizers such as multiple intelligence, learning styles, ethnicity, gender, children at risk, learning disabilities, critical thinking and brain research, the more precisely they will respond to the diverse needs of the learner" (p. 4). More importantly, they argue, "Action by any teacher in the absence of an intense connection to the reflection and actions of other professionals would be indicative of 'weak-sense' thinking" (Bennett & Rolheiser, 2001, p. 4). This provides a strong endorsement of the professional learning community model.

Common assessment—collaboratively designed and scored—lessens the divergence of instruction and therefore increases the integrity of classroom instruction.

High-quality assessment practice is equally specialized. We must be *assessment literate* (Stiggins et al., 2004), that is, conscious about using the appropriate method to match the learning target that the teacher has set for the class or individual student. Teachers who share in the development of common assessments help align curriculum outcomes and standards across grade and subject levels. As schools increasingly find themselves assigning teachers outside their area of subject expertise, developing common assessments will also increase teachers' professional knowledge of assessment methodology as well as subject expertise.

Bennett and Rolheiser (2001) make the point that there is clearly a number of ways to be equally effective and ineffective. Surely, the integration of the assessment process with the resulting changes in teacher methodology and behaviors will go a long way to create better learning chances for students. It is therefore incumbent for all teachers to make the necessary professional judgments in instruction based on sound assessment practices that will benefit the greatest number of their students through an informed, ethical, and collaborative approach.

Ongoing Professional Inquiry

There is so much to be said about this topic of common formative assessments. I have touched on only a few considerations and challenges teachers face in designing, administering, and marking these assessments, as well as in using the results to inform their teaching. The development and administration of common formative assessment has special meaning within the context of the professional learning community. As an instructional method, inquiry is a powerful way to engage students in deep learning. Why not use the same strategy to engage ourselves in discovering what each of us can do to answer the four critical questions of a professional learning community? By collaborating with each other and with our students to set, assess, and meet learning goals, and by using the body of knowledge about best instructional practices that has emerged, we can have a significant impact on student achievement.

References

Ainsworth, L. (2007). Common formative assessments: The centerpiece of an integrated standards-based assessment system. In D. Reeves (Ed.), *Ahead of the curve: The power of assessment to transform teaching and learning* (pp. 79–101). Bloomington, IN: Solution Tree.

Ainsworth, L., & Viegut, D. (2006). *Common formative assessments: How to connect standards-based instruction and assessment.* Thousand Oaks, CA: Corwin.

Bennett, B., & Rolheiser, C. (2001). *Beyond Monet: The artful science of instructional integration.* Toronto, Ontario: Bookation.

Black, P., & Wiliam, D. (1998). Inside the black box: Raising standards through classroom assessment. *Phi Delta Kappan, 80*(2), 139–148.

Blythe, T., Allen, D., & Powell, B. S. (1999). *Looking together at student work.* New York: Teachers College.

Butler, R. (1988). Enhancing and undermining intrinsic motivation: The effects of task-involving and ego-involving evaluation on interest and performance. *Journal of Educational Psychology, 58,* 1–14.

Cooper, D. (2007). *Talk about assessment: Strategies and tools to improve learning.* Toronto, Ontario: Thomson-Nelson.

Costa, A. L., & Kallick, B. (Eds.). (1995). *Assessment in the learning organization: Shifting the paradigm.* Alexandria, VA: Association for Supervision and Curriculum Development.

Davies, A. (2000). *Making classroom assessment work.* Courtney, British Columbia: Connections Publishing.

DuFour, R. (2007, October 10). *Common formative assessments and the question of pacing.* [Blog entry.] Accessed at www.allthingsplc.info on February 13, 2008.

DuFour, R., DuFour, R., Eaker, R., & Many, T. (2006). *Learning by doing: A handbook for professional learning communities at work.* Bloomington, IN: Solution Tree.

Hattie, J. A. (1992). Measuring the effects of schooling. *Australian Journal of Education, 36*(1), 5–13.

Marzano, R. J. (2000). *Transforming classroom grading.* Alexandria, VA: Association for Supervision and Curriculum Development.

Marzano, R. J. (2003). *What works in schools: Translating research into action.* Alexandria, VA: Association for Supervision and Curriculum Development.

Marzano, R. J. (2006). *Classroom assessment and grading that work.* Alexandria, VA: Association for Supervision and Curriculum Development.

McTighe, J., & Emberger, M. (2006, Winter). Teamwork on assessments creates powerful professional development. *Journal of Staff Development, 27*(1), 44.

Reeves, D. B. (2002). *The leader's guide to standards: A blueprint for educational equity and excellence.* San Francisco: Jossey-Bass.

Reeves, D. (2007). (Ed.). *Ahead of the curve: The power of assessment to transform teaching and learning.* Bloomington, IN: Solution Tree.

Sadler, D. R. (1998, March). Formative assessment: Revisiting the territory. *Assessment in Education, 5*(1), 77–84.

Saphier, J., & Gower, R. (1997). *The skillful teacher: Building your teaching skills.* Acton, MA: Research for Better Teaching.

Senge, P., McCabe, N. C., Lucas, T., Smith, B., Dutton, J., & Kleiner, A. (2000). *Schools that learn: A fifth discipline fieldbook for educators, parents and everyone who cares about education.* New York: Doubleday.

Stiggins, R. (2005). Assessment FOR learning: Building a culture of confident learners. In R. DuFour, R. Eaker, & R. DuFour (Eds.), *On common ground: The power of professional learning communities* (pp. 65–83). Bloomington, IN: Solution Tree (formerly National Educational Service).

Stiggins, R. (2007). Ottawa Assessment Institute.

Stiggins, R. J., Arter, J. A., Chappuis, J., & Chappuis, S. (2004). *Classroom assessment for student learning: Doing it right—using it well.* Portland, OR: Assessment Training Institute.

Teaching Effectiveness Program. (2000–2006). *Definition of assessment.* University of Oregon. Accessed at http://tep.uoregon.edu/workshops/teachertraining/learnercentered/assessing/definition.html on February 13, 2008.

Wiggins, G., & McTighe, J. (1998). *The understanding by design handbook.* Alexandria, VA: Association for Supervision and Curriculum Development.

Wiggins, G., & McTighe, J. (2005). *Understanding by design.* Alexandria, VA: Association for Supervision and Curriculum Development.

Wiggins, G., & McTighe, J. (2007). *Schooling by design: Mission, action and achievement.* Alexandria, VA: Association for Supervision and Curriculum Development.

SHARON V. KRAMER

Dr. Sharon Kramer knows firsthand the demands and rewards of working in a professional learning community. She served as assistant superintendent for curriculum and instruction of Kildeer Countryside School District 96 in Buffalo Grove, Illinois. In this position, she ensured all students were prepared to enter Adlai Stevenson High School, a model PLC created by the school's former superintendent, Dr. Richard DuFour. In addition her extensive experiences in urban, suburban, elementary, and unit school districts have shaped her vision of success for all students. Dr. Kramer is an "educator's educator" with a clear understanding of what it means to be involved in a collaborative culture that relies on frequent common formative assessments to improve learning. She earned her doctorate in educational leadership and policy studies from Loyola University of Chicago.

NINE

An Integrated Response to Learning: Eight Strategies That Work

Sharon V. Kramer

It has been said that teachers are second only to air traffic controllers in the number of decisions they make per minute. In any classroom, hundreds of decision-making events occur throughout the day. The greatest challenge in this environment of perpetual motion is ensuring that all students are learning. Teachers across North America are continually searching for better, more effective ways to ensure learning for all, despite the reality of academic diversity that exists in each classroom. Students have a wide range of knowledge, abilities, and academic needs—even in classes in which they have been sorted and selected by set criteria. In addition, teachers face curriculum overload and a maze of teaching strategies. Translating the curriculum and selecting teaching strategies to create instruction that ensures all students are learning is definitely a formidable task.

Out of necessity and time constraints, teachers often revert to teaching to the middle range of students, then reteaching to the whole class rather than the specific students who need more time and support. Carol Ann Tomlinson argues, "It is wrong to teach to the middle because struggling students miss out on important skills and knowledge while more able students are held back" (2006, p. 32). The way to avoid both traps, she says, is effective differentiation in mixed-achievement groups: to create "classrooms in which all students work with high-level, engaging, meaning-making curriculum in a flexible classroom environment" (p. 32). In such settings, says Tomlinson, "teachers would routinely provide support for students who need additional scaffolding to succeed with meaningful curriculum and for students who need to work at a more complex level. In other words, such classrooms would raise both the floor of expectations and the ceilings of possibility" (p. 32).

This chapter presents a strategic response to student learning that integrates interventions and enrichment to ensure that all students are learning. Through a collaborative process, teacher teams use assessment results to measure and manage each student's learning in order to provide the appropriate curriculum and instructional strategies. Teams share responsibility for student learning and create a system of support for all students. This collaborative, systematic response provides prevention, intervention, and acceleration to answer two essential PLC questions: "How will we respond when students do not learn?" and "How will we respond when students have already learned the essential knowledge and skills?"

Classroom Reality

In every classroom, there are *some* students who will need a little extra time and support to reach standards and a *few* students who will need more intensive challenges, supports, and interventions. There are also students who already know *some* of the concepts and knowledge contained in the standards and a *few* students who have a deep understanding of the standards. To the degree that students have different knowledge and learning needs, they each need a different instructional approach. Figure 9-1 illustrates this point. Students can be anywhere on the continuum below or above the core standards. The question is, "How can teachers create a strategic response to each student's learning to provide an appropriate level of challenge for all?"

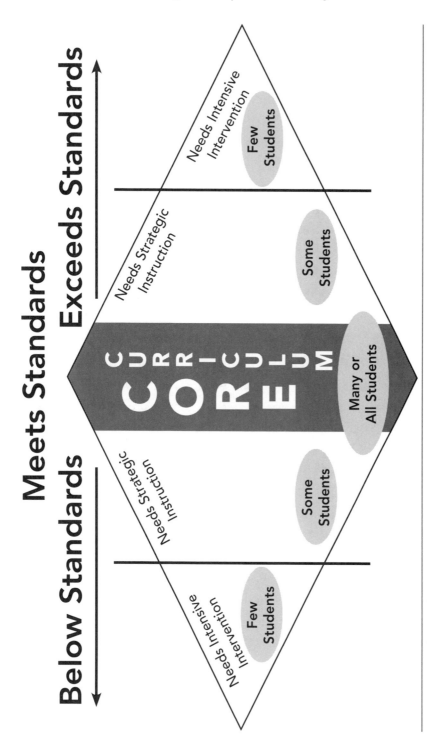

Figure 9-1: Student Achievement Reality in Our Classrooms

In a professional learning community, a pyramid of intervention provides a systematic response to students who need more time and support to learn. A PLC also provides targeted enrichment strategies to students who demonstrate that they already know some or all of the concepts. In this systematic approach, teachers differentiate instruction on an ongoing basis, and interventions and enrichment are seen as two sides of the same coin.

Assessing Classroom Reality

Formative assessments are defined as "all those activities undertaken by teachers and by their students [that] provide information to be used as feedback to modify the teaching and learning activities in which they are engaged" (Black & Wiliam, 1998, p. 140). An instructional system that ensures learning for all begins with a common formative preassessment to determine student needs.

Too often we teach curriculum from beginning to end with no consideration of students' prior knowledge. In this lock-step approach to learning, all curricula are treated equally. A preassessment allows teachers to make choices in order to focus on the areas of greatest need. In other words, it gives teachers permission to treat the curriculum unequally—to focus on *only* those specific essential knowledge and skills that students need to learn. Most textbooks include 4 to 6 weeks of review from the previous grade level or course. In the absence of common preassessment results, teachers are left to review most or all of the knowledge and skills from the past year. Using preassessment information, teachers can plan more effectively for whole and small group instruction to review only what is necessary, without wasting teaching time—which has been described as the scarcest resource in schools across the country. In addition, we send students the message that we expect them to retain and apply their prior knowledge as soon as they begin a new school year.

Common formative preassessments not only identify those students who may struggle to learn the essential standards, they also identify students who already know some or all of the standards—about 5 to 10% of students in a classroom. These bright students do not need to work hard to get good grades, and for them, the curriculum is probably too easy and requires little or no effort. According to Sylvia Rimm (1995) every student needs to experience the correlation between effort and results. When learning is usually easy, students never have the opportunity to struggle to learn. They rarely equate effort with learning and often become frustrated when they do not know the answer immediately. Eventually some bright students give up or find themselves struggling because they have not really learned how to learn. The goal of any curriculum should be to provide appropriate challenge so that all students put forth effort to learn.

In the traditional instruction-assessment model, we often begin with a preassessment, then teach an entire unit of study. Then we administer a post-test and assign grades. Unfortunately, the results usually show that while some students learned, a few students need more time and support to understand the concepts. Others already knew the material and spent the unit merely watching others learn. Whatever learning results the post-test shows, due to time constraints and the sheer amount of curriculum, the teacher usually moves on to the next unit of study. The students who did not learn the previous unit receive more instruction. It is not realistic, at this point, to expect that a student who did not learn the content the first time will be able to learn the new unit *and* catch up on the previous unit. How can the student keep up with the class when he is already behind? This practice of moving on before all students have learned creates a cycle of remediation in which most students struggle, some never catch up, and those who already knew the material watch and go nowhere.

A teacher using the instruction-assessment model that is focused on learning also begins with a pretest, but then she analyzes the results to create a plan for differentiated instruction, to strategically focus her teaching on student needs. Throughout the unit, like her colleagues, she frequently checks for student understanding using common formative assessments that provide the information needed to modify, reflect, and adjust instruction. At the end of the unit, teachers administer the post-test. Grades are assigned only after students have had sufficient opportunities to learn at their own challenge level—without the penalty of poor scores earned during the learning process. When instruction is differentiated, bright students are not rewarded with good grades despite their lack of effort. Effort equals learning. If a student does not put forth effort, he most likely knew the concepts or skills before the unit was introduced.

In a professional learning community, teachers use information from common preassessments for planning instruction. This information, in combination with frequent common formative assessment results, helps individual teachers and collaborative teams adjust instruction and provide interventions and enrichment for students at the point of need, rather than after the unit of study is over. When students are provided more time and support early enough, they are better able to keep up with grade and course expectations. In addition, this model ensures appropriate challenge in the curriculum for those students who already knew some or all of the essential standards.

A system of assessment that supports learning for all students provides a moving picture of each student's progress by incorporating common formative preassessments with short-cycle formative assessments throughout a unit of study. Common formative assessments play a critical role in scaffolding instruction for students. As Paul Black and his coauthors (2003) explain, "Formative assessments range from the questions teachers ask during class to how they mark written assignments. Such during-the-year assessments answer teachers' constant question: 'What should I do next?' They provide the feedback teachers need to adjust instruction and target struggling students" (p. 6).

How Do We Respond When Students Don't Learn?

A school can't become a professional learning community until it determines how it will respond when students do not learn (DuFour, DuFour, Eaker, & Many, 2006). In a professional learning community, a pyramid of interventions provides a systematic response to students who are not learning. An intervention is a specific response to student learning; it can be short or long term. It addresses the needs of students who require more time and support to learn, as well as those who just need encouragement to get their work done. In other words, interventions for the *can't do* and *won't do* students are different, but both are a part of the pyramid. A typical pyramid of interventions is comprised of three tiers of intervention ranging from least to most intensive (see Figure 9-2). Tier 1, the base level, is simply classroom-based instruction focused on the essential standards. In Tier 1, individual teachers use flexible grouping for differentiation of instruction with frequent progress monitoring.

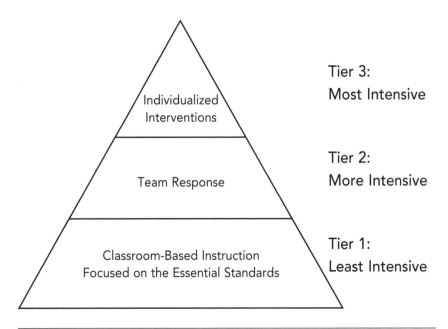

Figure 9-2: Pyramid of Interventions

In Tier 2, the middle level, a collaborative team responds to student learning needs. Teams of teachers review the results of the common formative assessments and group students for instruction or assign them to a schoolwide system of interventions based on need. These interventions are *in addition to* classroom learning, not in place of classroom learning. Participation in Tier 2 interventions is targeted and fluid. Students are grouped for specific knowledge or skills. For example, a student would not be given more time and support to learn the entire unit on fractions. Instead, the student would be given more support to learn about the specific skill of reducing fractions or adding fractions that he did not understand. The intervention is linked to the *specific* essential learning. In this manner, interventions are more fluid. Students are more motivated to participate when they know specifically what they need to learn.

Tier 3 interventions are tailored to individual needs. Most often, they involve one-to-one tutoring or other specially designed instruction—again, in addition to, not in place of, classroom learning. Intervention strategies in all tiers are monitored and evaluated based on their impact on student learning using results of common formative assessments and other indicators.

The pyramid of interventions is a systematic response that gives more time and support to students who are struggling to learn and keep up with their grade-level peers. It answers the question: "How will we respond when students do not learn?" Although it has proven successful for students who aren't learning, it does not address the needs of students who already know some or all of the essential outcomes for a given unit of study.

How Do We Respond When Students Have Already Learned?

If there is anything less scientific than a one-size-fits-all curriculum, I'm not sure what it might be.

—Richard Allington

Intelligent grouping maintains the same hopes and expectations for all students but recognizes where they are on a learning continuum (Wiggins, 2006). There are two important measures of student achievement. Teachers are all too familiar with proficiency measures; these include state and national assessments that measure whether a student has met or exceeded a certain cut score or bar. Growth measures such as the Northwest Evaluation Association's MAP (Measures of Academic Progress) tests are equally important because they determine whether students are growing or learning. Both measures are needed.

Many bright students meet proficiency standards but are not growing because they already knew all or part of the curriculum being tested. In most classrooms, there are students who know some or all of the essential outcomes. These students are often the most neglected group of students. They spend instructional time waiting for the others in class to catch up—no matter how much repetition of instruction is necessary. If we believe that all learners need appropriate challenge in the curriculum so that they must put forth effort to learn, then what is our systematic response for students who already have the knowledge and skills to move forward?

If we think of a pyramid of enrichment as having three distinct tiers much like the pyramid of interventions, Tier 1 would be the universal individual teacher response to enrichment (see Figure 9-3, page 188). This might take the form of deleting already mastered material from the existing curriculum, adding new content, process, or product expectations to existing curriculum, or extending existing curriculum to provide enrichment activities. In Tier 2, students who have already mastered the curriculum would be referred to a collaborative team for a schoolwide system of response. The team might teach tiered lessons, cluster group students for instruction, provide coursework at an earlier age than usual, or write new units or courses that meet the needs of advanced learners. Finally, in Tier 3, teachers would create an individualized student plan by creating contracts for learning, providing appropriate independent study materials, or allowing students to skip grades or enter advanced courses sooner than usual.

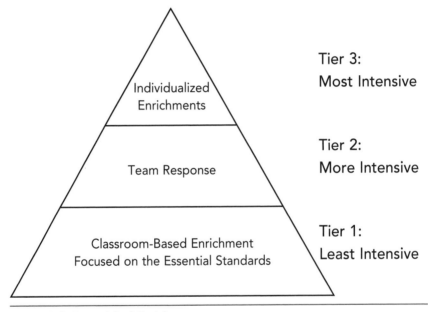

Figure 9-3: Pyramid of Enrichment

The pyramid of enrichment is a systemic response that allows all students to learn and grow. But the question that plagues most teachers is, "How can I meet all of these levels of learning in *one* class, given the obvious time constraints?"

An Integrated Approach

The research is clear: The most promising strategy to increase student achievement is for schools to function as professional learning communities. Collaborative teams have been described as the engine that drives a professional learning community (DuFour, DuFour, Eaker, & Many, 2006). When teachers are a part of collaborative teams focused on learning, student achievement levels increase. Collaborative teams understand that their fundamental purpose is to ensure high levels of student learning. Teachers on these teams know that to achieve their purpose, they need to work together, because it is impossible to accomplish if they work in isolation. Teams share responsibility for the learning of all the students at a grade level or in a specific course. Through the collaborative efforts of a team, the diverse educational needs of each student *can* be met during the instructional day.

Meeting the needs of all students does not imply that schools need to add new staff; instead, existing staff members may be repurposed or take on an expanded role. To meet student learning needs in a timely fashion, many professional learning communities expand their collaborative grade-level or subject-area teams to include other staff, such as special education resource teachers, ELL teachers, gifted teachers, reading specialists, teaching assistants, Title I staff, learning center staff, and technology teachers. The team problem-solves, plans instruction, and flexibly groups students. This collaborative approach creates a strong sense of shared responsibility for learning. These teams view students as an entire group—"all third graders in our school" or "all students taking Algebra I"—and analyze results of common formative preassessments together. This makes possible an integrated response that focuses on meeting the needs of all learners.

The integrated model does not replace or supplant good daily classroom instruction. In fact, it is based on individual classroom intervention strategies to identify the student's learning stage and apply the appropriate level of instruction. An integrated model allows the team to scaffold the regular classroom instruction.

The following eight examples show how different schools have developed and implemented integrated responses to student learning that provide prevention, intervention, and acceleration.

Example 1: Grade 4 Math Integrated Response

The teachers in a California elementary school were disappointed with the low math performance of their fourth-grade students on the state proficiency test. To improve their results, the fourth-grade teachers decided to pace the math standards and teach the exact same concepts each week. In addition, they decided to check for understanding by administering a short five-problem assessment at the end of every Thursday. After school on Thursdays, the fourth-grade team met for 10 minutes and did what they referred to as "shuffling the deck." They separated the papers from each of their classes into three stacks: all correct or one problem wrong, two or three problems incorrect, and four or five incorrect.

On Friday, they grouped students for instruction according to their scores on the check test from the day before. Students who had all the problems correct or one wrong were given an enrichment activity that extended their knowledge. Students with the lowest scores were grouped for reteaching using a different strategy. Students in the middle with some wrong answers did a check-for-understanding activity that reviewed the concepts in the lesson. Each week the teachers varied the group that they met with so that they each had an opportunity to work with all of the fourth graders.

Example 2: Elementary Schoolwide Response

A Wisconsin elementary school uses short-cycle checks for understanding to group students for instruction twice weekly. Each grade level designates two periods as "SMART time." During SMART time, teachers group students for interventions, review, or enrichment. Each grade level determines the subject area that will be the focus of their SMART time, based on the greatest area of need as identified in grade-level assessment data.

Example 3: Elementary School Expanded Team Model

The third-grade scores in a California school indicated that a quarter of the students were below grade level in reading. The third grade had 120 students with four teachers, for a student-teacher ratio of 30 to 1. To meet the varied needs of their students, the third-grade teachers expanded their team to include the reading specialist, one reading assistant, the special education resource teacher, the gifted/enrichment teacher, the ELL teacher, a Title I instructional assistant, and the learning center director. This expanded team planned additional instruction in reading to supplement regular classroom reading instruction, based on common formative assessments and biweekly progress monitoring.

The expansion of the team lowered the student-teacher ratio to 11 to 1. The students were divided into five groups for instruction. The most effective teachers were assigned to the neediest students, and the teachers were divided among the groups unevenly to provide a lower student-teacher ratio for the most struggling students:

- Group 1 was most intensive and had the lowest student-teacher ratio at 3 to 1.

- Group 2, the intensive group, had a 7 to 1 student-teacher ratio.

- Group 3, the less intensive group, had a 12 to 1 student-teacher ratio.

- Group 4, the grade-level group, had a 15 to 1 student-teacher ratio.

- Group 5, the advanced group, had a 35 to 1 student-teacher ratio.

Similar models have also been implemented in other schools to improve achievement in math and writing.

Example 4: Early Intervention Prevention Approach

An early childhood kindergarten center in Illinois has developed a program called the Vitamin Approach. Teachers in this half-day kindergarten provide daily reading instruction to their students. In addition, a team consisting of the teacher, the reading specialist, and two reading assistants deliver small group instruction in reading twice a week. Utilizing a centers approach, the teachers assign students to instructional groups based on an analysis of their assessment results. Some students are grouped for guided reading instruction, while others learn letters of the alphabet. In this way, each student receives an extra "dose" of reading—an educational vitamin. The kindergarten center's vision is for all students to be reading or ready to read by the end of their kindergarten school year.

Example 5: An Intervention, Prevention, and Acceleration Model

Team Read is based on the premise that the best intervention is prevention. This early intervention model for reading is implemented in kindergarten through grade 2 to prevent reading difficulties in later grade levels, when the focus will shift from learning to read to reading to learn. This prevention model is gaining in popularity due to its positive impact on achievement. The team uses common formative assessment results to group all students for additional reading instruction Monday through Thursday. The team is comprised of the classroom teacher, reading specialist, reading instructional assistant, and one other teacher; this additional teacher might be the ELL teacher or special education resource teacher, depending on the makeup of the class. Each class receives one half hour of instruction 4 days per week. The team uses the fifth day for planning. Student learning is monitored every 2 weeks, and instructional groups are adjusted according to the results.

Example 6: Preassessment as Early Warning System

A consortium of elementary schools in Illinois has developed a series of math preassessments for each unit of instruction. The preassessments are used to identify students who will need extra support—before they have a chance to fail. Teachers administer a common preassessment before each math unit of instruction. They score assessments by essential standard to measure each specific skill in the unit. Then the grade-level team meets with the math assistant and the enrichment teacher to analyze the results of the preassessment. The classroom teacher uses the data to focus instruction on those standards that the students do not understand. Students who have a score of at least 90% are included in the enrichment group for instruction. In addition, the students with the lowest scores on the pretest are grouped for extra instruction on specific skills with the math assistant. Students graph their own progress by standard on the pre- and posttests. They understand what they need to work on specifically and are anxious to report their progress, no matter where they scored on the pretest.

Example 7: Middle School Schoolwide Response

After reading the research on the positive correlation of nonfiction reading and writing on student achievement, teachers in a middle school in Louisiana instituted a daily 30-minute enrichment period that focuses on those strategies. During the enrichment period, students read high-interest expository books, articles, and periodicals on a variety of subject areas. (Students are surveyed to determine their interests, and every attempt is made to include topics that they suggest.) Students then apply the strategies they learn in their writing and content-area classes.

During the same period, students who need more time and support to learn—as indicated by assessments on specific standards in the curriculum—are assigned to a resource room for small group work.

The school has created a schedule of interventions for each day of the week, focusing on geometry one day and on English at a grade level the next. This ensures that the students are receiving instruction on the specific knowledge and skills that they need. It also provides time for students to get help in more than one subject.

Example 8: High School Model of Acceleration, Intervention, and Prevention

All students at this Illinois high school are held to rigorous standards. In fact, this school eliminated all of the remedial courses and replaced them with college preparatory courses. The school goal each year is to increase the percentage of students in each graduating class who complete a college-level course (Advanced Placement, dual credit, and articulated credit courses). To achieve this goal, the school eliminated the process of sorting and selecting students for advanced courses. Instead, each student who successfully completes the prerequisite course is encouraged to enroll in the next level. In this way, the school sees itself as opening future opportunities for all students.

This expectation of acceleration for all is supported by strong pyramid of intervention strategies. The school recognizes that to meet its goal, some students will need more time and support. Teachers issue progress reports every 3 weeks and report cards every 6 weeks. Any student who is in danger of failing (receiving a D or an F) is monitored weekly. Intervention strategies include multidisciplinary resource centers, mandatory tutoring, guided study hall, and a mentor program that structures and monitors progress toward graduation on an individual basis.

As a part of the prevention initiative, teachers also instituted a freshman watch program to prevent failure by students at risk. In addition, a freshman mentor program matches upperclassmen with freshman to ensure a smooth social transition to high school for each student throughout the first year. This model of acceleration, intervention, and prevention provides students with unlimited opportunities and the support needed to meet the rigorous expectations and standards set by the teachers.

Creating an Integrated, Responsive System

An integrated system that responds to student learning is based on the following action steps. These steps are ongoing for each unit of study.

- Identify essential standards.

- Determine what each standard means, and agree on what achievement of these standards would look like.

- Pace the standards, and cluster them in a unit of study.

- Develop the common postassessment.

- Based on the postassessment, create the common preassessment.

- Administer the preassessment.

- Review the results.

- Plan instruction and flexibly group students.

- Monitor progress with short-cycle formative measures.

- Regroup students for intervention or enrichment based on the results of the formative measures.

- Administer the formative postassessment.

- Group students for interventions and enrichment based on the results.

Often educators assume that long-standing traditional practices are "best" practices. This assumption does not encourage teachers to imagine the possibilities. Consider these questions:

- What can you do to address the needs of all learners in your classroom? (individual possibilities)

- What can a team of teachers do to address the needs of all learners? (collaborative possibilities)

- What can the school do to address the needs of all learners? (schoolwide possibilities)

An integrated response to learning calls for teachers to think beyond what we have always done in the past. Students who struggle to learn and students who demonstrate that they already know the essential standards need a response to their learning that supports their specific needs. It is nearly impossible, given the academic diversity and time constraints in each class, for a single teacher to be all things to all students. Meeting the needs of all students requires an integrated response that utilizes all the resources and support available in a school. It truly takes teams working interdependently to solve problems, revise, reflect, and adjust instruction to educate every student. Collaboration is the key to measuring and managing student learning to ensure that all students are both meeting proficiency standards and growing.

References

Ainsworth, L., & Viegut, D. (2006). *Common formative assessments: How to connect standards-based instruction and assessment.* Thousand Oaks, CA: Corwin Press.

Allington, R. (2005, June/July). The other five "pillars" of effective reading instruction. *Reading Teacher, 22*(6), 3.

Black, P., Harrison, C., Lee, C., Marshall, B., & Wiliam, D. (2003). *Assessment for learning: Putting it into practice.* New York: Open University Press/McGraw Hill.

Black, P., & Wiliam, D. (1998, October). Inside the black box: Raising standards through classroom assessment. *Phi Delta Kappa, 80*(2), 139–147.

Conzemius, A., & O'Neill, J. (2001). *Building shared responsibility for student learning.* Alexandria, VA: Association for Supervision and Curriculum Development.

DuFour, R., DuFour, R., Eaker, R., & Karhanek, G. (2004). *Whatever it takes: How professional learning communities respond when kids don't learn.* Bloomington, IN: Solution Tree (formerly National Educational Service).

DuFour, R., DuFour, R., Eaker, R., & Many, T. (2006). *Learning by doing: A handbook for professional learning communities at work.* Bloomington, IN: Solution Tree

Olson, L. (2004, February 25). ETS imports "formative assessment" analyst. *Education Week, 23*(28), 6–7.

Landrum, M. (2002). *Consultation in gifted education: Teachers working together to serve students.* Mansfield Center, CT: Creative Learning Press.

Rakow, S. (2007, August). All means all: Classrooms that work for advanced learners. *Middle Ground, 11*(1), 10–12.

Rimm, S. (1995). *Why bright kids get poor grades: And what you can do about it.* New York: Three Rivers Press.

Tomlinson, C. (1999). *The differentiated classroom: Responding to the needs of all learners.* Alexandria, VA: Association for Supervision and Curriculum Development.

Tomlinson, C. (2003a). *Differentiation in practice: A resource guide for differentiating curriculum grades K–5.* Alexandria, VA: Association for Supervision and Curriculum Development.

Tomlinson, C. (2003b). *Differentiation in practice: A resource guide for differentiating curriculum grades 5–9.* Alexandria, VA: Association for Supervision and Curriculum Development.

Tomlinson, C. (2006, April). An alternative to ability grouping. *Principal Leadership (Middle Level Edition), 6*(8), 31–32.

Wiggins, G. (2006). *Voices: The contrarian.* Accesssed at www.essentialquestions.org on November 15, 2006.

MARY ANN RANELLS

Dr. Mary Ann Ranells is a public speaker, trainer, author, and award-winning practitioner with over 35 years experience as an educational professional. The principal of Silver Hills Elementary in Wallace, Idaho, Dr. Ranells provides strong leadership by using research-based school improvement methods. Dr. Ranells has worked as a classroom teacher, deputy superintendent, and director of curriculum and instruction. She has often played a key role in aligning curriculum to meet state standards, and she has directed Title I and other federal programs in Idaho and Washington school districts. A four-time recipient of Teacher of the Year awards, Dr. Ranells has also been honored with the Idaho Association of School Administrators (IASA) Leadership in Public Education Award and Nampa (Idaho) School District Teacher Foundation Award. She is a member of the Association for Supervision and Curriculum Development, IASA, and Phi Delta Kappa, among other organizations.

A New Era of Spectacular Teachers

Mary Ann Ranells

As Deputy Superintendent for a state Department of Education, when I first heard of No Child Left Behind, I thought its intent was noble. Like every professional educator, I had long dreamed that every teacher would be highly qualified and that every student would meet rigorous academic standards. As the new law began to consume most activities at the state level, I watched as legislators, administrators, and school board members frantically revisited policies and requirements for licensure. Meanwhile, classroom teachers made Herculean efforts to implement the new state content standards, administer the new high-stakes state testing program, and meet accountability require-ments. As Nichole, a fantastic fifth-grade teacher explained at the time, "We were accustomed to chipping away at continuous improve-ment; now it feels like we are hammering."

As I traveled from one end of the state to the other in an attempt to provide technical assistance to educators as they valiantly imple-mented the new framework, I gained insight into the chasm between the assumption inherent in the *ideal* of highly qualified and the *appli-cation* at the "shop-floor" level. After listening to the successes and frustrations of teachers across the state, I knew I needed to return to the classroom to learn from my colleagues and to experience first-hand what worked and what didn't.

Little did I know the journey to gaining certification in another state would teach me the real meaning of *highly qualified*. Interestingly, obtaining an administrator's certificate only required filling out the necessary application forms, requesting official transcripts, and sending in the check. But to obtain certification as a highly qualified teacher, my four degrees and 32 years of experience were inadequate; I also had to take a test to prove myself worthy to step into the classroom.

I taught Spanish in a small rural high school, where I also served as the district's "Director of Et Cetera": special education, Title I, federal programs, staff development, curriculum, and state assessments. There I learned a powerful lesson: the difference between highly qualified teachers and *spectacular* teachers. Teachers who meet their states' definitions of "highly qualified" under the NCLB Act do not necessarily teach in ways that ensure students will meet the academic standards. At best, NCLB requirements show that teachers have met the qualifications for entering the classroom—not that they have demonstrated their effectiveness in that classroom (Darling-Hammond, Holtzman, Gaitlin, & Heilig, 2005).

There have always been spectacular teachers, but there are significant differences in what they do now and what they did 20 years ago to help students achieve at high levels.

Spectacular teachers in today's classrooms are more focused and intentional in the following ways:

- They build relationships.
- They collaborate with colleagues to design learning systems.
- They redesign grading practices.
- They wear multiple hats.
- They create a legacy for future generations.

A professional learning community framework not only helps us remember and utilize best practice for learning, collaboration, and results (DuFour, DuFour, Eaker, & Many, 2006), but also lays a fortified foundation that allows us to keep improving over time. Spectacular teachers are doing the right things. The ongoing discourse between these colleagues reaches new levels of intensity as they describe expectations in terms of student performance, analyze understandings and misunderstandings, and determine adjustments needed to close the achievement gap. They breathe life into the "highly qualified" rhetoric through a continuous focus on learning.

Spectacular Teachers Build Trusting Relationships

In *Trust in Schools,* Anthony Bryk and Barbara Schneider (2002) study the importance of social relationships to student learning and achievement. "Schools," state the authors, "are networks of sustained relationships. The social exchanges that occur and how participants infuse them with meaning are essential to a school's functioning" (p. xiv). In nationwide efforts to raise standards and improve student learning and achievement, trust is the key ingredient at the school level: "[A] broad base of trust across a school community lubricates much of a school's day-to-day functioning and is a critical resource as local leaders embark on ambitious improvement plans" (p. 5). The relationship between teachers and administrators relies on a level of trust that breeds confidence. This confidence translates into feelings of safety and security, allowing both teachers and administrators to take risks without fear of reprisal. It's a feeling of "I've got your back, and I know you've got mine." But it goes beyond this. There is an *expectation* of honest feedback for improvement. After observing Jennifer, a new teacher with several years of experience, I felt compelled to write a letter to her describing the excellence in teaching and learning I had witnessed in her classroom. Shortly after she had received my letter, she stormed into my office and told me how furious she was that I had not given her one idea for improvement—

and she knew I always had ideas for teachers. We had a remarkable discussion about the level of trust necessary for her to expect more from me and me from her. Trust is also key on the classroom level: "Trusting student-teacher relationships are essential for learning" (Bryk & Schneider, 2002, p. 31).

Get to Know Students

Spectacular teachers go about forming personal bonds with students in many ways. Each year, for example, Brad, an eighth-grade social studies teacher, asks his students to introduce themselves to the class. After the last student is finished, Brad shakes each student's hand, says his or her name out loud, and cheerfully adds, "I'm really happy to meet you!" Students are astonished that he can remember all their names on the first day. He then passes out index cards and asks students to provide their name, address, phone number, birthday, hobbies, interests, and what they hope to get out of the class.

Finally, Brad groups the students according to how many years they have been in the school or school district by 5-year increments and asks them to answer a series of questions about their school experiences. They tell candid stories about elementary school disasters, junior high pranks, and high school pride. Deal and Peterson would call this "historicizing" (1994). In listening to their stories, Brad begins to understand what students value. He also shares stories about himself; students ask about his family, what he has done in the past, if he likes teaching, and what he thinks of kids. This helps them know what he values. Brad said he always wants to know students personally and to have them know him as a first step in building trusting relationships.

Solicit Student Perspectives

Forming trusting relationships creates shared values and allows teachers to share their expectations in a way that is significantly different than merely explaining classroom rules. Sylvia, an incredible sixth-grade teacher, creates shared values with the following exercise. She provides a handout divided into four sections labeled "My Job Is," "My Job Is Not," "Your Job Is," and "Your Job Is Not." Students fill in ideas for each quadrant from their perspective as a student, and Sylvia fills one out from her perspective. Once the handout is completed, the class shares ideas and compiles similarities and dissimilarities on their perceptions of the responsibilities of teachers and students.

Sylvia reported students felt her job was to be fair, to be consistent, and to make learning fun. They thought it was very important for her to keep them posted on where they were as each grading period progressed. They didn't want to be surprised when report cards came out. Her job was not to have favorites, assign busy work, or tolerate inappropriate behavior. Their job was to pay attention, participate, get their homework done, and study for tests. Their job was not to cheat, complete mindless assignments, or sit through boring lectures. "Inviting students to share their opinions," she explained to me, "sends the message I want them to hear: I value and respect their ideas."

Provide Structure

Routines, procedures, ceremonies, and rituals provide the parameters of teachers' and students' expectations—students know what to expect of themselves, each other, and the teacher. Maureen, a kindergarten teacher, reported how clear structure, organization, and natural consequences created a "love and logic" environment in her classroom (Fay, 1998). During guided discussion groups, Maureen and her students agree on classroom rules and consequences for following the rules or not following the rules. "Every year I have to resist the urge to just give them my list of rules," she confessed to me, "but I've seen a big difference in attitude and behavior between classes where students participated in setting the rules and consequences and those that did not." She also has students role-play appropriate and inappropriate behaviors during activities such as reading aloud, working in small groups, taking tests, eating lunch, attending an assembly, and so on. Students even create their own behavior rubrics so they know if they are functioning effectively as a class. Effort, participation, attendance, being on time, all become part of their feedback system. Of course, this is also the lady who exclaimed, "This is so exciting. I can't believe I get paid to do this!"

Engage Students in the Learning Process

One strategy for creating trusting relationships with students that is surprisingly significant is teaching the students *how* we teach. A department of English teachers annually instructs students on the teaching model and evaluation tool for effective teaching and learning they had adapted as a school. They explain to the students that this is important in order for them to be able to communicate with the teachers about what they understand, and, more importantly, about what they don't understand. They teach students the principles of learning (such as motivation, retention, transfer, making meaning, and so on), describe the teaching models they use most often, and explain metacognition and Bloom's Taxonomy. One teacher said she will never forget the day a student named Marc raised his hand and asked, "Isn't this a secret?"

The good news about teaching students how we teach and how we expect them to learn is that students become actively engaged in their learning. The bad news is that spectacular teachers end up having evaluators of their teaching everyday! The English teachers said some days it is more than a little frustrating to hear comments such as the following:

"Excuse me, what is the objective?"

"We aren't ready for independent practice."

"The activity doesn't match the objective."

"I don't think there is a positive feeling-tone in the room today."

As painful as it may be on some days, according to these teachers, this particular routine does create a learning environment of continuous improvement for the students and for them—an essential component of working as a professional learning community.

Show Respect and Interest

A critical aspect of nurturing trusting relationships is a constant focus on respect. Students challenge us frequently to see if what we call appropriate behavior for them is also how we act. A spectacular teacher consistently models the expected behavior even when pushed. Modeling is the most important adult behavior in the classroom. If we don't show students respect under trying circumstances, we cannot expect them to show us respect.

In *The Art and Science of Teaching* (2007), Robert Marzano responds to the question, "What will I do to establish and maintain effective relationships with students?" in the opening paragraphs by offering the following:

Arguably the quality of the relationships teachers have with students is the keystone of effective management and perhaps even the entirety of teaching. There are two complementary dynamics that constitute an effective teacher-student relationship. The first is the extent to which the teacher gives students the sense that he is providing guidance and control both behaviorally and academically. In effect, the teacher must somehow communicate the message: "You can count on me to provide clear direction in terms of your learning and in terms of behavior. I take responsibility for these issues." The second dynamic is the extent to which the teacher provides a sense that teacher and students are a team devoted to the well-being of all participants. In effect, the teacher must somehow communicate the message: "We are a team here and succeed or fail as a team. Additionally, I have a stake personally in the success of each one of you." (p. 149)

Teachers report their greatest challenge continues to be the fight against student apathy and are almost disheartened that a miracle cure has not been discovered. But what they do find effective is a demonstrated, genuine interest in the lives of the students as individuals. If teachers take the time to go to their games, recitals, and concerts, students act differently toward the teachers. It doesn't seem to matter if the students have supporting families or if they are pretty much on their own. Something almost magical happens when students know their teachers care enough about them to be there to support them. Students are better in class, more persistent when learning new knowledge, and more apt to tell teachers when they don't understand. Something that costs nothing except time yields incredible results. Building strong relationships takes time, energy, and follow-through, and the benefits are priceless.

Spectacular Teachers Collaborate to Design Learning Systems

Extraordinary teachers are doing things very differently these days when it comes to designing a system for learning. Teachers collaborating in a team structure focused on student learning is possibly the biggest change since the 1990s. As Fiske (1992) points out, "To truly reform American education we must abandon the long-standing assumption that the central activity is teaching and reorient all policy making and activities around a new benchmark: student learning" (p. 253). This is the core shift we make in becoming a professional learning community.

It's almost impossible to hide out anymore. Teachers can no longer go into their classrooms, shut the door, and hope this PLC and collaboration business will all go away. Lickona and Davidson (2005) found that:

Great schools "row as one"; they are quite clearly in the same boat, pulling in the same direction in unison. The best schools we visited were tightly aligned communities marked by a palpable sense of common purpose and shared identity among staff—a clear sense of "we." By contrast, struggling schools feel fractured; there is a sense that people work in the same school but not toward the same goals. (p. 65)

As collaboration becomes the norm, teachers across all grade levels and content areas take an iterative approach to creating a learning system by examining the state standards, state tests, and local tests. Teachers are "backloading" high-stakes testing requirements into their pacing guides and have incorporated math, writing, and reading skills in subjects outside the core for two important reasons: 1) These concepts and processes represent excellent ways to demonstrate acquisition of subject-matter knowledge; and 2) students are counting on all the adults in a school to do their duty-bound best to prepare them to be successful. Whether state tests are deemed representative of what students should know, do, and understand doesn't seem to be as important now as what the focus on these tests has done to cause teachers to come together to talk about students and their learning.

Four Critical Questions for Collaboration

DuFour, DuFour, Eaker, and Many (2006) encourage teachers to answer four critical questions:

1. What knowledge and skills should every student acquire as a result of this unit of instruction?

2. How will we know when each student has acquired the essential knowledge and skills?

3. How will we respond when some students do not learn?

4. How will we respond when some students have clearly achieved the intended outcomes? (p. 21)

Teachers working together to answer these questions have found it essential to dig deeper into *knowing* than merely reviewing the state standards and saying, "I teach that." Today a high school diploma means that students are literate—math literate, science literate, language arts literate, and more—as evidenced by their demonstration of proficiency on the standards. Spectacular teachers have found it necessary to focus on some standards more than others to make certain all students will master the essential knowledge, skills, and dispositions necessary to be successful at the next level (Reeves, 2005).

Based on these "power standards," spectacular teachers collaboratively create pacing guides, common assessments, and establish proficiency targets. This process helps learning teams become very intentional in their teaching, it provides a platform for monitoring student progress, and it leads to consistency in grading practices.

Collaborating With Students

Students are part of a professional learning community and its focus on learning. Spectacular teachers engage students in the language of learning by connecting the learning goals to the performance measures. Students are able to determine what their brains have to do to show they understand. They can verbalize the differences in learning targets that are specific to knowledge mastery, reasoning, skills or processes, or creating products (Stiggins, Arter, Chappuis, & Chappuis, 2006). In the past, the learning targets were clear to the teacher, but the student just knew the assignment or test had to be completed. The synergetic relationship between the learning goal and the assignment was not readily apparent. Now teachers are making certain students can describe what is to be learned in terms of what they are asked to do. When students can identify the standards they are learning and where their performance is in relation to the standards, teachers stand a much better chance of providing quality feedback.

John Hattie (1992) reviewed 7,827 studies on learning and instruction and concluded, "The most powerful single innovation that enhances achievement is feedback. The simplest prescription for improving education must be 'dollops' of feedback" (p. 9). Providing students with specific information about their standing in terms of particular objectives increased their achievement by 37 percentile points (Marzano, Pickering, & Pollock, 2001). Spectacular teachers provide timely, accurate feedback that encourages students to try again. If students know where they are in relation to a target and they know what they have to do to reach the target, it's amazing what they will do to achieve the goal.

Providing ongoing quality feedback means that spectacular teachers must give students a second chance to improve their performance (Guskey, 1997)—not for everything that is taught, but for those power standards we feel are critical to student success. Spectacular teachers regularly allow students multiple attempts at learning and involve students in tracking their growth.

Many learning teams are utilizing best practices regarding feedback as part of their pyramid of interventions (DuFour, DuFour, Eaker, & Many, 2006). The power of the professional learning community framework provides the schoolwide structure necessary to monitor student progress in a relentless manner. The daily schedule includes additional time and support for students. Spectacular teachers don't accept excuses; they don't tolerate mediocrity; and they are more stubborn than the students. This isn't to say that all students will meet all expectations, but the design certainly increases the chances of success.

Another dimension that has significantly changed is the integration of technology in the classroom. Whether teachers use it to keep track of student progress, to better communicate with parents and guardians, or to enhance learning, the tapestry of knowledge acquisition is constantly changing in texture and brilliance. This is true for the system of learning in general as well; the design evolves as teachers focus on what students are learning as a result of instruction.

Spectacular Teachers Redesign Grading Practices

The entire arena of grading and reporting has improved in great teachers' classrooms. Students are no longer surprised by the grade they receive or why they received it. They are more confident that an A in one teacher's classroom means pretty much the same thing in another teacher's classroom. More and more teachers are abandoning averaging as a way to evaluate overall student performance.

Teachers know that for the most part, it is easy to create a new report card. Unfortunately, a new report card format doesn't fundamentally change the way we teach and the way children gain understanding. According to Marzano (2006), the research on grading reveals the following truths:

- Grading is not essential to the instructional process.

- Grading is complicated.

- Grading involves some degree of subjectivity.

- Grades have some value as a reward, but no value as a punishment.

- Grading and reporting should always be done in reference to learning criteria, never "on the curve."

Spectacular teachers have tackled the most sacred of old traditions and are developing ways to communicate more accurately what is in a grade and what it means. Learning Teams begin this phase of the journey to becoming a PLC by addressing the following seven steps (Marzano, 2006).

Step 1: Decide Whether Classroom Grading Should Change

I had the opportunity to work with four separate school districts on creating standards-based reporting systems. The Learning Teams (organized by grade level, department, vertical level, and so on) have reported the current system is akin to educational malpractice. They contend the inconsistencies in grading practices alone should be cause enough to address the issue (Marzano, 2006). Some teachers said they based grades purely on student achievement, while others included nonacademic factors such as behavior and getting homework in on time. For spectacular teachers, if the learning system is dependent on the scaffolding from one level to the next, agreement on what should be learned, what learning that knowledge should look like, and determining how good is good enough should be non-negotiable.

Step 2: Clarify the Purpose of Grading and Reporting

Teachers are becoming more and more expert at utilizing formative information as part of the learning process and summative information to identify student performance at certain points in time. The overall agreement seems to be that grading and reporting should be used as feedback to students and parents and should inform practice.

Step 3: Determine What Will Be Included in Grades

Teacher Learning Teams begin with the end in mind. After re-examining their state standards, required test objectives, and any other district-required curriculum, they meet with teachers of students in the grade level or course above them and the grade level or course below them to identify the essential knowledge, skills, and dispositions students should master. A critical piece of this process is to examine examples of measures the teachers use to judge student mastery. This constitutes the heart and soul of determining what goes into a grade. In reviewing standards-based or standards-referenced report cards, teachers include at least two categories: academic achievement and behavior. They identify the criteria, the performance, and the measures for each and report on them separately. They delineate academic achievement further by the following categories:

- Knowledge or concept attainment

- Skills or processes

- Thinking and reasoning

- Products

- Communication

When we weigh what should be included in a grade, we should ask ourselves: What does learning this knowledge require students to demonstrate? What will we accept as credible evidence that students have learned what we wanted them to learn at the level we think is good enough?

Nonacademic indicators might include effort, participation, attendance, turning in homework on time, and so on. Determining the criteria for acceptable performance is just as critical for nonacademic behaviors as it is for academic. This is most evident in observing daily schedules, routines, rituals, and interactions. The Bruneau-Grandview School District (a small rural school district) staff agreed on the nonacademic indicators to be included in the report card, created a rubric for each one, and included grades for these separate from the academic grades. Perhaps even more amazing was that they used the same rubrics for kindergarten through 12th grade. Expectations were clear and graded consistently from year to year, teacher by teacher.

Step 4: Decide How to Track Achievement on Each Standard

In a professional learning community, teacher teams design classroom assignments and assessments tied to standards and performance objectives. They continually refine the description of what learning will look like in terms of student performance. They collaborate on what types of measures, assessments, and targets will be acceptable for determining progress toward the year-end standards. They identify growth expectations along the way to better monitor and communicate student progress. Teachers report this is generally the stage in the process where they determine what the grade book should include. For example, one fifth-grade Learning Team made up of 27 teachers across seven elementary schools decided the grade book would include two components of writing: organization of ideas and mechanics/usage. They assigned five essays for the quarter, utilized the same rubric for scoring, scored the papers as a team, and entered the scores in the grade books. Final grades were not averaged. The teachers determined the current performance level and assigned grades accordingly.

Interestingly, we don't hear much about "teaching to the test" anymore. The dialogue is more along the lines that if we feel this concept, skill, process, or reasoning skill is imperative to future learning and understanding, we don't care if it's on the test—the kids should be able to demonstrate mastery regardless.

Step 5: Students Identify Their Learning Responsibilities

Teacher teams agree on strategies they will incorporate that require students to share in the responsibility of their learning goals by keeping track of their progress, behaviors, and individual goals. Students personalize learning goals by identifying something they would like to know or do in relation to the objective and help establish the criteria for meeting that target. More and more teachers are utilizing student-led conferences, which is good, but our daily practices have more impact than an occasional conference. When students keep track of their own growth toward a predetermined target, it's amazing to see what can happen (Ainsworth & Viegut, 2006). Self-evaluation based on strong and weak models gives students a sense of control and hope. If we use the fifth-grade writing example mentioned previously, students were given anchor papers scored according to an analytical rubric and were asked to work in small groups to score their own essays similarly. Students quickly learned where their performance was in relation to the target, and quality feedback gave them the confidence they could improve over time and meet the target. They began to believe in themselves and their own efficacy as they set their own goals and monitored their progress toward those goals.

Step 6: Gather the Evidence

This is probably the most difficult phase of the process, and one that has no ending. In a professional learning community, teacher teams grade assignments and assessments collaboratively in order to create consistent grading policies. Sometimes we are amazed to discover the vast differences in our personal definitions of acceptable work. Even more profound are the differences in our criteria. For instance, some teachers will give more weight toward neatness than actual understanding of the concept, skill, or product. Answering the question, "How good is good enough?" is critical for teachers at this point. This step also forces teachers to address the process for calculating and assigning a final grade. Is an A in one class equivalent to an A in another class? Spectacular teachers engage in lengthy processes to determine if their grading is accurate, fair, and consistent.

Step 7: Compare With Other Sources of Data

Many teachers report that comparing their results to state tests, advanced placement tests, district level assessments, and so on isn't something they've done in the past. Spectacular teachers take the time to review other sources of data, however, to see if the grades they're giving reflect student performance on state and national tests.

Teaching practices related to grading and reporting are going through a type of extreme makeover from a focus on what is being taught to what is being learned. What is being learned is consistent from one teacher to the next, and an A in one classroom is the same as an A in another classroom. Spectacular teachers know this alignment process is essential if every child is expected to meet the academic standards as a condition of receiving a high school diploma.

Spectacular Teachers Wear Multiple Hats

Great teachers have always gone above and beyond the call of duty, but it seems their involvement in the school and community has tripled. In addition to teaching, many teachers coach or perform in an advisory capacity for various clubs and organizations. They serve on short- and long-term committees, function as department heads, and assume roles for coordinating a myriad of state and federal programs. They write grants, participate in a variety of professional development opportunities, and often become in-house trainers for programs being implemented in the school or district. They believe in stewardship and connect with parents and the community on a number of levels. Some participate in PTO, some are volunteer firefighters, and others belong to community-based organizations. They deal with a literal mountain of paperwork, complete many reports and surveys, and spend hours on data entry and data analysis.

These incredible leaders explain how important it is to them to be involved beyond the classroom. They have a better sense of the "big picture" and like to have a voice in selecting the colors of paint being used to create that big picture.

Spectacular Teachers Create a Legacy for Future Generations

Many people will recall the NASA Teacher in Space Program and the tragedy of the Challenger in 1986. Barbara Morgan, an elementary school teacher from McCall, Idaho, was the substitute for Christa McAuliffe and witnessed that sorrowful event. Twenty years later, on August 8, 2007, Barbara was part of the shuttle crew for the Endeavour STS-118 mission. As the space shuttle broke free and surged toward the stars, the announcer on the television said, "Barbara

Morgan, racing toward space on the wings of a legacy. Class is in session." What a remarkable tribute to teachers around the world, and what an incredible legacy to leave behind.

Today's teachers, like Barbara, are creating a legacy for future generations in which students can realize their talents and fulfill their destinies. In order to leave this legacy behind, spectacular teachers model organization, execution, passion, and persistence. They believe in the unlikely and can make the abstract concrete. They challenge the status quo by seeing possibilities instead of barriers. They don't need to think outside of the box, because there is no box for them. They create victories for children everyday and keep hope alive. They genuinely care about each and every child and fan the flames of desire to excel. For these teachers, there is no minimum bar. Their courage, devotion, and selflessness inspire and jolt us out of complacency. Being highly qualified is a good place to begin, but becoming a spectacular teacher makes our profession truly worthy of respect and keeps us dreaming.

Returning to the classroom to work side by side with colleagues determined to make a difference in the lives of children profoundly changed the way I think and behave as a teacher and an administrator. I will be forever grateful to these amazing, spectacular heroes for helping me learn to never be satisfied with the status quo and to always strive to be better tomorrow than I was today.

References

Ainsworth, L., & Viegut, D. (2006). *Common formative assessments: How to connect standards-based instruction and assessment.* Thousand Oaks, CA: Corwin.

Bryk, A. S., & Schneider, B. (2002). *Trust in schools: A core resource for improvement.* New York: Russell Sage Foundation.

Collins, J. (2001). *Good to great: Why some companies make the leap . . . and others don't.* New York: HarperCollins.

Darling-Hammond, L., Holtzman, D. J., Gatlin, S. J., & Heilig, J. F. (2005). *Does teacher certification matter? Evidence about teacher certification, Teach for America, and teacher effectiveness.* Chapel Hill, NC: The Southwest Center for Teaching Quality.

Deal, T. E., & Peterson, K. D. (1994). *The leadership paradox: balancing logic and artistry in schools.* San Francisco: Jossey-Bass.

DuFour, R., DuFour, R., Eaker, R., & Many, T. (2006). *Learning by doing: A handbook for professional learning communities at work.* Bloomington, IN: Solution Tree.

Erwin, J. C. (2004). *The classroom of choice: Giving students what they need and getting what you want.* Alexandria, VA: Association for Supervision and Curriculum Development.

Fay, J. (1998). *Love and logic: How to create a love and logic classroom.* Golden, CA: Love and Logic Institute, Inc.

Fiske, E. (1992). *Smart school, smart kids: Why do some schools work?* New York: Simon and Schuster.

Guskey, T. R. (1997). *Implementing mastery learning.* Belmont, CA: Wadsworth Publishing.

Guskey, T. R. (2001). *Developing grading and reporting systems for student learning.* Thousand Oaks, CA: Corwin.

Hattie, J. (1992). Measuring the effects of schooling. *Australian Journal of Education, 36*(1), 5–13.

Hattie, J., Biggs, J., & Purdie, N. (1996). Effects of learning skills interventions on student learning: A meta-analysis. *Review of Educational Research, 66*(2), 99–136.

Lickona, T., & Davidson, M. (2005). *Smart and good high schools: Integrating excellence and ethics for success in school, work, and beyond.* Cortland, NY: Center for the 4th and 5th R's (Respect and Responsibility), and Washington, DC: Character Education Partnership.

Marzano, R. J. (2006). *Classroom assessment and grading that work.* Alexandria, VA: Association for Supervision and Curriculum Development.

Marzano, R. J. (2007). *The art and science of teaching: A comprehensive framework for effective instruction.* Alexandria, VA: Association for Supervision and Curriculum Development.

Marzano, R. J., Pickering, D., & Pollock, J. E. (2001). *Classroom instruction that works: Research-based strategies for increasing student achievement.* Alexandria, VA: Association for Supervision and Curriculum Development.

Reeves, D. (2005). Putting it all together: Standards, assessment, and accountability in successful professional learning communities. In R. DuFour, R. Eaker, and R. DuFour (Eds.), *On common ground: The power of professional learning communities* (pp. 45–63). Bloomington, IN: Solution Tree.

Stiggins, R., Arter, J., Chappuis, S., & Chappuis, J. (2006). *Classroom assessment for student learning: Doing it right—Using it well.* Portland, OR: Educational Testing Service.

The Collaborative Administrator
Austin Buffum, Cassandra Erkens, Charles Hinman, Susan Huff, Lillie G. Jessie, Terri L. Martin, Mike Mattos, Anthony Muhammad, Peter Noonan, Geri Parscale, Eric Twadell, Jay Westover, and Kenneth C. Williams
Foreword by Robert Eaker
Introduction by Richard DuFour
In a culture of shared leadership, the administrator's role is more important than ever. This book addresses your toughest challenges with practical strategies and inspiring insight.
BKF256

Learning by Doing: A Handbook for Professional Learning Communities at Work™
Richard DuFour, Rebecca DuFour, Robert Eaker, and Thomas Many
The second edition of this pivotal action guide includes seven major additions that equip educators with essential tools for confronting challenges. **BKF416**

The Power of Professional Learning Communities at Work™: Bringing the Big Ideas to Life
Featuring Richard DuFour, Robert Eaker, and Rebecca DuFour
This video series explores eight diverse schools, where teachers and administrators engage in candid conversations and collaborative meetings. See how successful schools radically improve student learning as you learn the fundamentals of PLC. **VIF094**

Revisiting Professional Learning Communities at Work™: New Insights for Improving Schools
Richard DuFour, Rebecca DuFour, and Robert Eaker
This 10th-anniversary sequel to *Professional Learning Communities at Work™* offers advanced insights on deep implementation, the commitment/consensus issue, and the human side of PLC. **BKF252**